Microsoft Expression® Design on Demand

Ted LoCascio

QUE®

Que Publishing
800 East 96th Street
Indianapolis, IN 46240 USA

Microsoft® Expression® Design on Demand

Library of Congress Cataloging-in-Publication Data
LoCascio, Ted.
  Microsoft Expression Design on demand / Ted LoCascio.
      p. cm.
  Includes index.
  ISBN 0-7897-3826-0
  1. Computer graphics. 2. Microsoft Expression Design. I. Title.
  T385.L618 2008
  006.6'86—dc22

                                            2008006818

  ISBN-13: 978-0-7897-3826-4
  ISBN-10: 0-7897-3826-0

Printed and bound in the United States of America
First Printing: April 2008

11 10 09 08   4 3 2 1

Que Publishing offers excellent discounts on this book when ordered in quantity for bulk purchases or special sales.

For information, please contact: U.S. Corporate and Government Sales

   1-800-382-3419 or corpsales@pearsontechgroup.com

For sales outside the U.S., please contact: International Sales

   1-317-428-3341 or International@pearsontechgroup.com

Trademarks

Warning and Disclaimer

Publisher
   Paul Boger

Associate Publisher
   Greg Wiegand

Acquisitions Editor
   Loretta Yates

Development Editor
   Laura Norman

Managing Editor
   Gina Kanouse

Technical Editor
   Aaron Jasinski

Project Editor
   Andy Beaster

Page Layout
   Gloria Schurick

Interior Designers
   Steve Johnson
   Marian Hartsough

Indexer
   Lisa Stumpf

Proofreader
   Betsy Harris

Team Coordinator
   Cindy Teeters

Acknowledgements

Ted LoCascio

First and foremost, I must thank everyone at Que Publishing and Perspection for making this book possible. Thanks to associate publisher Greg Wiegand and to acquisitions editor Loretta Yates for sharing my vision on this project and for being as genuinely enthusiastic about Expression Design as I am. Thanks also to development editor Laura Norman for helping me organize this title and paying such close attention to the details, and to Aaron Jasinski for acting as my technical editor and making sure every step, shortcut, and tip are correct.

Special thanks to my proofreader, Betsy Harris, for making this book read as well as it does. I must also thank my project editor, Andy Beaster, for working with me on the book's schedule and keeping everything on track.

Loving thanks to my wife, Jill, and to my son, Enzo, for being so patient while I was busy writing this book. Thanks also to Mom, Dad, Val, Bob and Evelyn Innocenti, and the rest of my extended family for being so supportive.

I must also thank Lynda Weinman, Tanya Staples, and the rest of the wonderful staff at Lynda.com for allowing me to be a part of their excellent online instructor team and for being so much fun to work with.

I would also like to thank CreativePro.com and the *InDesign Magazine* staff, especially Terri Stone and David Blatner. Special thanks also go out to Barry Anderson, Mordy Golding, and all the instructors and staff at the Mogo Media Conferences.

And, of course, thanks to the Microsoft Expression development team for making such great software to write about.

Dedication

To my wonderful wife, Jill, and our son, Enzo, for their never-ending love and support.

About the Author

Ted LoCascio is a professional graphic designer, author, and educator. He served as senior designer at the National Association of Photoshop Professionals (NAPP) for several years and has created layouts, graphics, and designs for many successful software training books, videos, websites, and magazines. Ted is the author of numerous graphics software training books and has contributed articles to *Photoshop User* magazine, Creativepro.com, the *Quark Xtra* newsletter, PlanetQuark.com, and *InDesign Magazine*. He has also taught at the Adobe CS Conference, the InDesign Conference, the Pixel Conference, the Vector Conference, and PhotoshopWorld. He is also the author of numerous graphics software training videos, all of which are available at www.lynda.com. A graphic designer for more than ten years, Ted's designs and illustrations have been featured in several national newsstand and trade magazines, books, and various advertising and marketing materials. For more about Ted LoCascio, please visit http://tedlocascio.com.

We Want To Hear From You!

As the reader of this book, *you* are our most important critic and commentator. We value your opinion and want to know what we're doing right, what we could do better, what areas you'd like to see us publish in, and any other words of wisdom you're willing to pass our way.

As an associate publisher for Que, I welcome your comments. You can email or write me directly to let me know what you did or didn't like about this book—as well as what we can do to make our books better.

Please note that I cannot help you with technical problems related to the topic of this book. We do have a User Services group, however, where I will forward specific technical questions related to the book.

When you write, please be sure to include this book's title and author as well as your name, email address, and phone number. I will carefully review your comments and share them with the author and editors who worked on the book.

Email: feedback@quepublishing.com

Mail: Greg Wiegand
        Que Publishing
        800 East 96th Street
        Indianapolis, IN 46240 USA

For more information about this book or another Que title, visit our website at *informit.com/register*. Type the ISBN (excluding hyphens) or the title of a book in the Search field to find the page you're looking for.

This Book Is Safari Enabled

The Safari® Enabled icon on the cover of your favorite technology book means the book is available through Safari Bookshelf. When you buy this book, you get free access to the online edition for 45 days. Safari Bookshelf is an electronic reference library that lets you easily search thousands of technical books, find code samples, download chapters, and access technical information whenever and wherever you need it.

To gain 45-day Safari Enabled access to this book:

◆ Go to *http://www.informit.com/onlineedition*

◆ Complete the brief registration form

◆ Enter the coupon code **58EV-KTHC-IY5D-BICG-853R**

If you have difficulty registering on Safari Bookshelf or accessing the online edition, please e-mail customer-service@safaribooksonline.com.

Contents

Introduction

Welcome to *Microsoft Expression Design on Demand*, a visual quick reference book that shows you how to work efficiently with Expression Design. This book provides complete coverage of basic to advanced Expression Design skills.

How This Book Works

You don't have to read this book in any particular order. We've designed the book so that you can jump in, get the information you need, and jump out. However, the book does follow a logical progression from simple tasks to more complex ones. Each task is presented on no more than two facing pages, which lets you focus on a single task without having to turn the page. To find the information that you need, just look up the task in the table of contents or index and turn to the page listed. Read the task introduction, follow the step-by-step instructions in the left column along with the screen illustrations in the right column, and you're done.

Step-by-Step Instructions

This book provides concise step-by-step instructions that show you how to accomplish a task. Each set of instructions includes illustrations that directly correspond to the easy-to-read steps. Also included in the text are time-savers, tables, and sidebars to help you work more efficiently or to teach you more in-depth information. A "Did You Know?" provides tips and techniques to help you work smarter, whereas a "See Also" leads you to other parts of the book containing related information about the task.

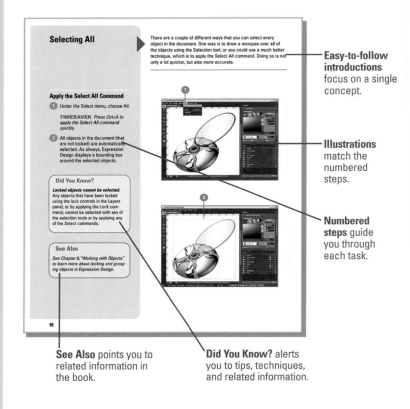

Easy-to-follow introductions focus on a single concept.

Illustrations match the numbered steps.

Numbered steps guide you through each task.

See Also points you to related information in the book.

Did You Know? alerts you to tips, techniques, and related information.

Sample Files

This book uses the sample files that are installed with Expression Design to give you a context in which to use each task. You can locate these files by navigating on your system to the Program Files\Microsoft Expression\Design\Samples folder. By following along with the sample files, you won't waste time looking for or creating your own assets. Note that not every task requires a sample file, such as "Drawing with the Pen Tool." In these instances, you will perform the task from scratch.

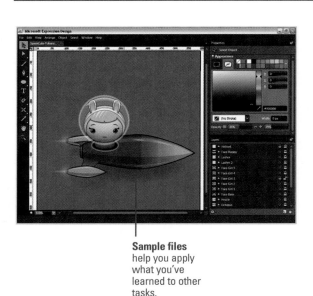

Sample files help you apply what you've learned to other tasks.

Get Updates

Like any software, Expression Design continues to change and get better with updates and patches, so it's important to regularly check the Microsoft Expression Design site at *www.microsoft.com/products/ expression/*.

Get Updates for Expression Design online.

Expression Studio

Expression Design is part of the Microsoft Expression Studio, which also includes Expression Web, Blend, and Media. Expression Web is a professional design tool used to create websites that conform to modern standards-based sites on the web. Expression Blend is a professional design tool used to create engaging, web-connected user experiences for Windows. Expression Media is a professional asset management tool used to visually catalog and organize all your digital assets for effortless retrieval and presentation.

Expression Studio combines tools to create an expanded development environment.

Getting Started with Expression Design

Introduction

Microsoft Expression Design is a powerful illustration tool that allows you to create both vector and bitmap graphics for use in projects created with the other applications in the Studio suite, including Expression Web and Expression Blend. It is only available for purchase as part of Expression Studio and not as a standalone application.

As a tightly integrated member of the Studio suite, Expression Design allows you to design custom web graphics and export them as GIFs or JPEGs for use in sites created with Expression Web. You can also use Expression Design to create custom user interface controls and export them in the native XAML format for use in interfaces created with Expression Blend.

In this chapter, you will learn the necessary steps for installing Expression Design on PCs running either the Windows XP or Windows Vista operating systems. (Expression Studio is currently not available for Mac OS X.) You will also learn to identify the basic items of the Expression Design interface, as well as how to open pre-existing documents and create new ones from scratch. Most importantly, you'll learn all about document page structure and how to control the size of your artboard and document.

Once you've mastered these basic fundamentals, you can move on to familiarizing yourself with the available panels and tools in Expression Design.

What You'll Do

Prepare to Install Expression Design

Install Expression Design

Launch Expression Design

Identify Expression Design Interface Items

Open a Document

Open Multiple Documents at Once

View Active Files

Create a New Document

Save a Document

Set Ruler Units

Set Ruler Origin

Change Document Size

Change the Artboard Size

View Artwork in Wireframe Mode

Preparing to Install Expression Design

System Requirements

Before you can install Expression Design, you must make sure that your computer meets the following system requirements:

Operating System:

- ◆ Microsoft Windows XP with Service Pack 2 (SP2)
- ◆ Windows Vista

Minimum System:

- ◆ Intel Pentium or AMD processor, 1 GHz with MMX or equivalent
- ◆ 512MB of RAM
- ◆ 150 MB available hard disk space
- ◆ 1024 x 768 monitor resolution with 24-bit color
- ◆ Graphics processor that is DirectX 9–capable

Recommended System:

- ◆ Intel Pentium or AMD processor, 2 GHz with MMX or equivalent
- ◆ 1 GB of RAM
- ◆ 600 MB available hard disk space
- ◆ Microsoft DirectX 9.0–capable video card with 256 MB or more of memory—for example, ATI Radeon X300 or NVIDIA GeForce 5600 class equivalent or better.

If you are not sure that your computer meets the minimum system requirements, you can find out by referring to the Windows XP or Vista System Information accessory. To do so, click the Start menu button in the taskbar, go to All Programs, Accessories, System Tools, System Information.

Install Microsoft .NET Framework First

If you are using Windows XP rather than Vista, you must install .NET Framework 3.0 *before* installing Expression Design. You can download the software for free at www.microsoft.com/downloads, or click the .Net Framework 3.0 link available in the Expression Studio CD set-up guide.

To install the software, double-click the installer icon and follow the instructions in the Setup Wizard.

Install Expression Design Service Pack 1

After you've installed Expression Design, you must update it by downloading and installing Expression Design Service Pack 1.

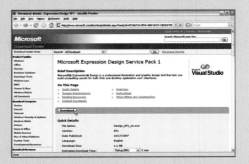

Installing Expression Design

Expression Design can only be purchased as part of the Expression Studio suite, which includes Expression Blend, Expression Web, and Expression Media. When you insert the Expression Studio installer CD, a setup guide automatically displays in your default web browser. You can use this guide to access the individual Expression Studio product installers. Use the following steps to install Expression Design onto your computer.

Install Expression Design

1 Insert the Microsoft Expression Studio CD into your drive.

The installer CD displays a set-up page in your default web browser. Click **Windows Vista** or **Windows XP,** depending on which operating system you are using.

◆ If the set-up page does not automatically appear in your browser, choose **My Computer** from the **Start** menu and double-click the **Microsoft Expression Studio** disc icon.

2 If you are using Windows XP, install .NET Framework 3.0.

3 Click the **Expression Design** button to access the installer and choose **Save File.** Navigate to the default download location on your system and double-click the installer icon.

4 The Microsoft Expression Design Setup Wizard appears. Click the **Next** button and follow the steps provided.

5 When the installation is complete, click **Finish** to exit the wizard.

Launching Expression Design

When you first open Expression Design, the default workspace panel arrangement is displayed. This includes the Layers panel and Properties panel (both docked on the right side of the screen) and the Tools (positioned on the left). The Action bar (the gray area at the bottom of the screen) is also open but remains blank until a document is opened and an item is selected. By default, a new document is not automatically opened when launching the application.

Start Expression Design Using the Start Menu

1 Click the **Start** button on the taskbar.

2 Point to **All Programs.**

3 Click **Microsoft Expression**.

4 Click **Microsoft Expression Design.**

5 In the window that appears, enter your product key and click **Continue.**

The Expression Design interface appears, displaying the default workspace panel arrangement.

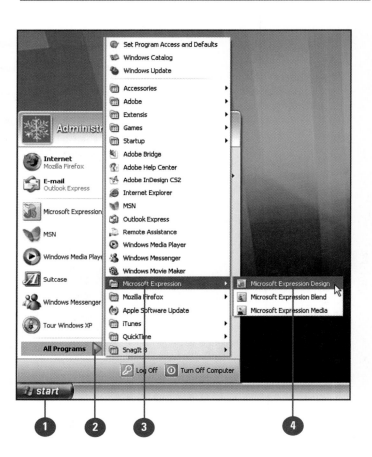

Identifying Expression Design Interface Items

Flip Bar   Menu Bar   Horizontal Ruler

Properties Panel

Tools

Vertical Ruler

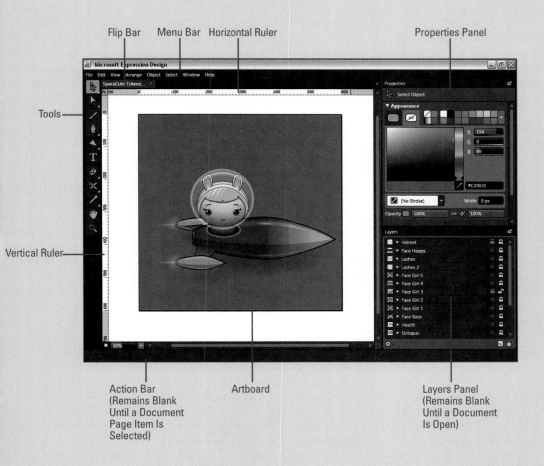

Action Bar
(Remains Blank
Until a Document
Page Item Is
Selected)

Artboard

Layers Panel
(Remains Blank
Until a Document
Is Open)

Opening a Document

Anytime you want to create artwork in Expression Design, you must do so within the confines of a document page. However, before you begin creating new documents, it helps to understand how to open pre-existing ones. Expression Design actually ships with some documents that are accessible through the Samples folder, which is installed along with the application. To access the Samples folder, navigate to the drive where you installed Expression Design; open the Program Files/Microsoft Expression/Design folder.

Choose the Open Command

1. Under the **File** menu, choose **Open**.

   TIMESAVER *Press Ctrl+O to apply the Open command quickly.*

2. In the Open File dialog box that appears, navigate to the file you'd like to open.

3. Select the filename and click **Open**. The document automatically appears in the work area of the interface.

Did You Know?

You can preview the document from within the Open File dialog box. To preview the document before you open it in Expression Design, check the Show Preview check box located in the lower left corner of the dialog box.

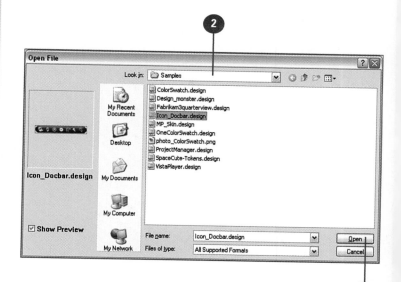

Opening Multiple Documents at Once

With Expression Design, you can also open multiple documents at once. This can be useful when working with multiple web graphics or interface items that are intended for use in much larger Expression Web or Expression Blend projects.

Select Multiple Files

1. Under the **File** menu, choose **Open.**

2. In the Open File dialog box that appears, navigate to the folder containing the files you'd like to open.

3. Shift+click to select adjacent filenames, or Ctrl+click to select nonadjacent files.

    IMPORTANT *You cannot preview multiple selected items in the Open File dialog box. When opening multiple files at once, Expression Design only allows you to preview one document at a time.*

4. Click **Open.** The documents automatically appear stacked in the work area of the interface.

5. Each document's name is displayed in a separate tab in the Flip bar. Click a tab to bring the corresponding document to the front.

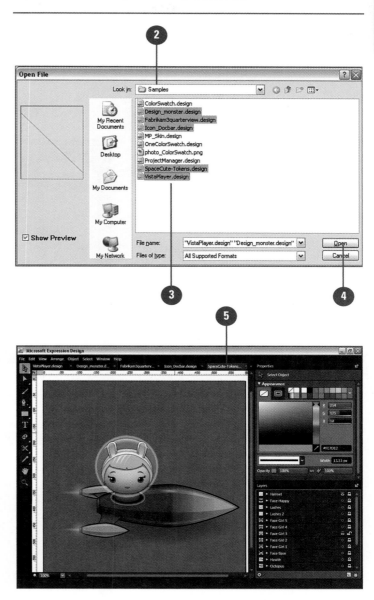

Viewing Active Files ▶

When you have multiple documents open, there are several different ways to control which one is currently being displayed. Expression Design contains a Flip bar at the top of the document window that displays the names of as many open documents as it can fit. By clicking the document name, you can bring it to the front of the stack. All open documents (including those not shown in the Flip bar) can be accessed via the active files list located under the Window menu, or via the Active Files menu to the far right of the Flip bar.

Choose the Document Name from the Window Menu

① You can view a numbered list of open documents under the **Window** menu. The current document has a check mark displayed next to its name.

② Select the name of the document you'd like to view.

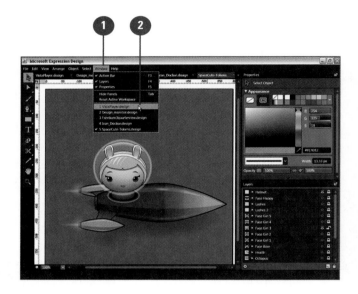

Click the Document Name in the Flip Bar

① Each document's name is displayed in a separate tab in the Flip bar. Click a tab to bring the corresponding document to the front of the stack.

TIMESAVER *Press Ctrl+Tab to view the next open document displayed in the Flip bar. Press Ctrl+Shift+Tab to view the previous document.*

Choose from the Flip Bar Active Files Menu

1 The Flip bar can only display a limited number of document tabs. If you know a document is open but do not see its name listed in the Flip bar, you can access it from the **Active Files** menu.

To access the menu, click the down arrow in the upper right of the document window, on the far right of the Flip bar. The current document has a check mark displayed next to its name.

2 Select the name of the document you'd like to view.

Did You Know?

You can only display one document at a time. Unfortunately, Expression Design does not contain a Tile feature that allows you to view multiple documents side-by-side.

Hovering over a document name in the Flip bar reveals the current file location. When you hover over any document tab in the Flip bar, a tooltip appears to display where the file is currently stored on your system.

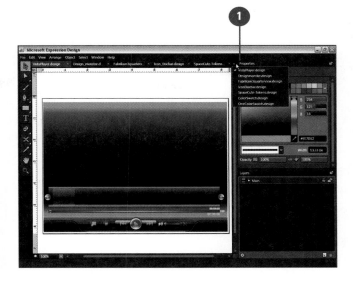

Creating a
New Document

To create graphics in Expression Design, you must first create a document. Every document contains a frame, also referred to as the "artboard," which determines the visible output area for your artwork. You can control the size of the document frame by entering specific width and height dimensions in the New Document dialog box. After the document is created, a black outline is displayed to indicate the position of the artboard. All the artwork that you intend to export or print should be placed within this area.

Choose the New Document Command

1 Under the **File** menu, choose **New**.

> **TIMESAVER** *Press Ctrl+N to apply the New Document command quickly.*

2 In the New Document dialog box that appears, choose a preset document size from the **Presets** list, or enter specific width and height values in the fields provided. Choose the preferred measurement units from the list provided. This also determines what units will appear in the document rulers.

3 If necesssary, change the resolution value from the default setting (96 ppi, which is the standard for onscreen display). Web graphics are generally saved at 72 ppi, and print graphics at a minimum of 220 ppi.

4 It is not necessary to name the file when setting it up in the New Document dialog box, but the option is there if you'd like to. You can always name the file later when saving it.

5 Click **OK** to create the new document.

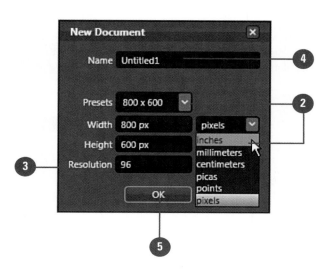

Saving a Document

As you work in Expression Design, you should periodically save your documents. Doing so allows you to preserve the work you've done and return to it later, even after you've closed the file. There's nothing worse than losing hours of hard work due to a power surge or unexpected system shutdown. Therefore, in addition to saving, you might also want to consider investing in a battery backup for your workstation.

Choose the Save Command

1 Under the **File** menu, choose **Save**.

> **TIMESAVER** *Press Ctrl+S to apply the Save command quickly.*

The **Save** command is only available when updating pre-existing documents—not when saving for the first time, which requires the use of **Save As**.

You should also use **Save As** to avoid overwriting an original document that you've applied changes to. Doing so creates a copy of the document and allows you to change its name and system location.

Choose the Save As Command

1 Under the **File** menu, choose **Save As**.

> **TIMESAVER** *Press Ctrl+Shift+S to apply the Save As command.*

2 Enter a name for the document in the **File Name** field of the Save As dialog box.

3 Choose a system location and click **Save**.

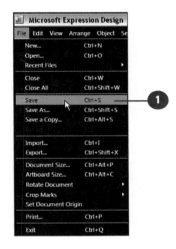

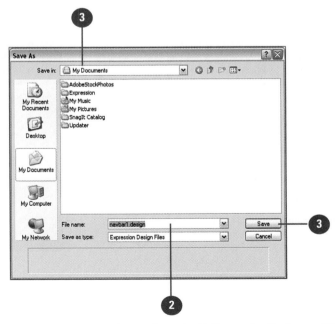

Setting Ruler Units

In addition to the artboard, every document also contains a set of rulers: one horizontal (top) and one vertical (left). Expression Design lets you decide which set of measurement units you'd like to display in the rulers. The Units and Grids Options include points, inches, millimeters, centimeters, picas, and pixels. Note that both rulers are always visible (there is no option to hide them), and that they both display the same measurement units.

Changing Document Ruler Unit Options

1 Under the **Edit** menu, point to **Options** and choose **Units and Grids** from the fly-out menu.

TIMESAVER *Press Ctrl+K to quickly access the Options dialog box. Select Units and Grids from the menu on the left.*

2 In the Options dialog box that appears, choose the preferred measurement units from the **Document Units** list.

3 Click **OK** to update the document rulers.

Did You Know?

You can specify measurement unit options when creating a new document. The New Document dialog box contains a Units list that allows you to determine what measurement units will be displayed in the document rulers.

You can easily identify what measurement units are currently applied. Expression Design displays a two-letter abbreviation for the currently selected unit option in the upper left corner of the document window (where the horizontal and vertical rulers meet).

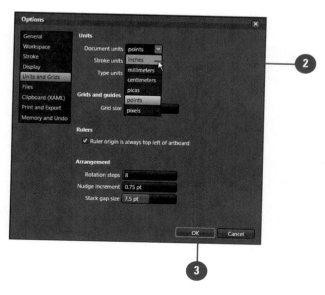

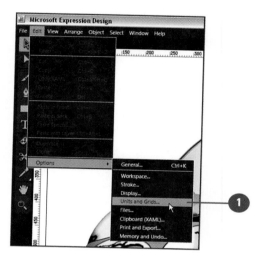

Setting Ruler Origin

The ruler point of origin, also referred to as the "zero point," is the location along the edge of the artboard where zero is positioned in the rulers. In Expression Design, you can choose to place the zero point for both rulers in the upper left corner of the artboard or place it in the upper left for the horizontal ruler and in the bottom left for the vertical ruler.

Changing the Ruler Origin Option

1 Under the **Edit** menu, point to **Options** and choose **Units and Grids.**

> **TIMESAVER** *Press Ctrl+K to quickly access the Options dialog box. Select Units and Grids from the menu on the left.*

2 In the Options dialog box that appears, uncheck **Ruler Origin Is Always Top Left of Artboard.** This changes the ruler origin for the vertical ruler from the upper left to the bottom left.

Did You Know?

The ruler origin follows your movements as you scroll. The gray area in both rulers indicates all values below zero. As you scroll through or zoom in and out of the document, the gray areas update themselves.

Did You Know?

You can also create a custom zero point. To create a custom zero point, choose Set Document Origin from the File menu and click and drag anywhere in the document. When you release the moue button, Expression Design resets the rulers.

Point of Origin

Point of Origin

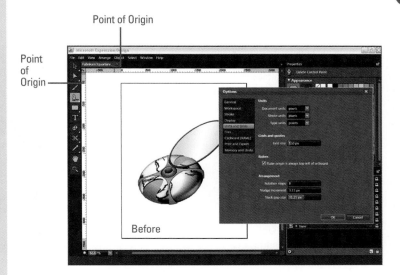

Before

Point of Origin

Point of Origin

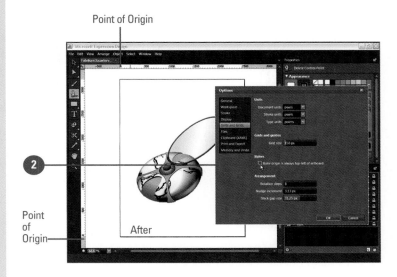

After

Changing Document Size

Anytime you need to change the overall size and/or resolution value of your artwork (for example, to resize a print graphic for use on the web), you can do so by using the controls available in the Document Size dialog box. Remember that any adjustments made using this method affect everything in the document, including the artboard and all your artwork.

Use the Document Size Dialog Box

1 Under the **File** menu, choose **Document Size**.

> **TIMESAVER** *Press Ctrl+Alt+P to quickly access the Document Size dialog box.*

2 Enter new width and height values in the fields provided. Check **Constrain Proportions** to resize the document proportionally. If necessary, you can select a different measurement unit from the list provided. Doing so also changes the units that are displayed in the rulers after the dialog box is closed.

3 If necesssary, change the resolution value from its current setting. Web graphics are generally saved at 72 ppi, and print graphics at a minimum of 220 ppi.

> **IMPORTANT** *The resolution value does not automatically update when adjusting document dimensions. Therefore—because the controls do not do the math for you—it is difficult to interpolate (resample) a bitmap graphic using the Document Size dialog box. Upsizing a low-resolution graphic might result in unwanted pixelation during output.*

4 Click **OK** to change the document size.

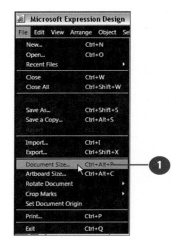

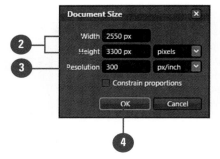

Changing the Artboard Size

If you'd like to resize the artboard *without* resizing your artwork, you can do so using the controls available in the Artboard Size dialog box. This allows you to extend your canvas and increase the output area or reduce it to crop away portions of your art.

Use the Artboard Size Dialog Box

1 Under the **File** menu, choose **Artboard Size**.

> **TIMESAVER** *Press Ctrl+Alt+C to quickly access the Artboard Size dialog box.*

2 Enter new width and height values in the fields provided. If necessary, you can select a different measurement unit from the list provided. Doing so also changes the units displayed in the document rulers after the dialog box is closed.

If you prefer, check the **Relative** option and enter the exact amount you would like to add to (or subtract from) the width and height of the artboard. Use negative values to subtract.

3 Click any of the arrows in the **Anchor** grid to control which sides of the artboard will be added to or subtracted from. To add or subtract evenly from the center, leave the anchor point at its default setting.

4 Click **OK** to change the artboard size.

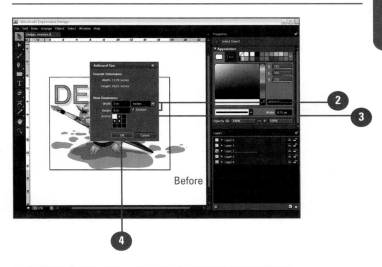

Before

Aft[er]

Viewing Artwork in Wireframe Mode

By default, Expression Design displays all documents in Preview mode, which reveals all applied attributes, such as fill colors, stroke colors, and effects. However, if you'd like to view the paths that make up the artwork without any attributes applied, you can do so by switching the Display Quality setting to Wireframe mode. This is a great way to take a look at what's going on "under the hood" of your artwork. Switching to Wireframe mode can also make it easier to locate specific paths that you'd like to select and edit, especially when working with detailed pieces of art.

Change the Display Quality Setting

1 Under the **View** menu, choose **Wireframe** from the **Display Quality** submenu.

TIMESAVER *Press Ctrl+Y to toggle between Preview and Wireframe modes.*

Expression Design displays the paths that make up the artwork without showing any applied fill and stroke colors or effects.

Did You Know?

Natural media brushstrokes remain visible in Wireframe mode. Natural media brushstrokes appear just as they do in Preview mode. The only difference is that the underlying path is revealed.

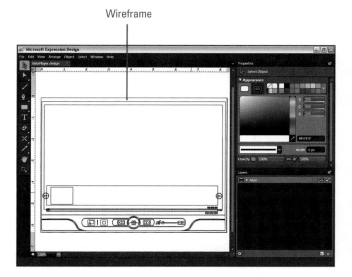

Wireframe

Working with Panels

Introduction

Like most software applications, the tools and controls in Expression Design are accessible through various panels. However, Expression Design is unique in that its interface contains only four panels. This is an extremely conservative interface structure and a welcome change in the world of creative software.

Two of the four panels in Expression Design are dynamic (the Action bar and Properties panel), which means that the controls they display are determined by the objects you've selected in the document as well as the tools you've chosen to work with.

The onscreen arrangement of the panels is what is known as the workspace. Expression Design allows you to dock two of the panels to the right side of the screen (the Properties panel and Layers panel). You can also expand the dock, hide and show panels, and reposition and resize floating panels onscreen (and resize them vertically in the dock). Expression Design also contains a command that allows you to reset the default onscreen panel arrangement, which is referred to as the Active Workspace.

The Tools panel in Expression Design is not as flexible as the other three because it does not allow you to undock, resize, or reposition it onscreen. However, identfying and selecting tools in the panel is easy with the help of tooltips.

In this chapter, you'll get comfortable with your new work environment by learning everything there is to know about panels.

What You'll Do

View Controls in the Action Bar

Show and Hide Panels

Resize the Dock

Float Panels

Dock Panels

Show and Hide Advanced Properties

Reset the Active Workspace

Select Tools

Identify Tool Shortcuts with Tooltips

Viewing Controls in the Action Bar

In the default onscreen panel arrangement (referred to as the Active Workspace in Expression Design), the Action bar is open but remains blank until you select any item in the document. After making a selection, the Action bar displays the current X and Y coordinates for that item (its current position in the document) as well as its width and height dimensions. There are also controls for rotating and skewing the object. When multiple items are selected, the Action bar also displays additional Align, Distribute, Stack, and Path controls.

Select Any Item in the Document

① Make sure the Action bar is visible by selecting **Action Bar** under the **Window** menu. If a check mark is currently displayed next to the words **Action Bar**, then it is already open.

> **TIMESAVER** *Press F3 to quickly hide or show the Action bar.*

② Select any item in the document with either the Selection tool or Direct Selection tool. Shift+click to select multiple items.

The Action bar displays the current X and Y coordinates and width and height dimensions for all selected items. It also includes Rotation Angle and Skew Angle controls. When multiple items are selected, the Action bar also displays additional Align, Distribute, Stack, and Path controls.

Did You Know?

If multiple items are selected, the Action bar also displays a set of Align, Distribute, Stack, and Path controls. Click any of these words to apply the default setting for each option. To access additional options, click the down arrow to the right of each control.

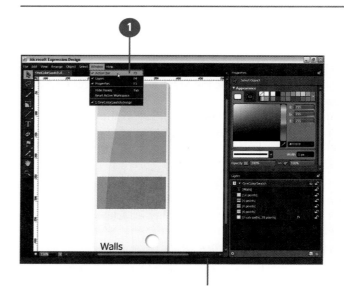

Action Bar (Remains Blank Until an Object Is Selected)

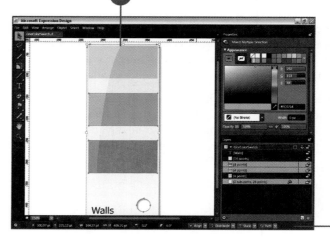

Action Bar

Showing and Hiding Panels

When it comes to eating up screen real estate with panels, Expression Design is extremely conservative. However, even though there are only four panels in the entire interface, there are still times when they can get in the way. If you need to make more room onscreen to focus on your artwork, you can close certain panels or hide all of them at once.

Choose the Window Commands

1. Under the **Window** menu, select **Action Bar**, **Layers**, or **Properties**. Expression Design displays a check mark next to each item that is currently open. The keyboard shortcut for each command is also displayed to the right of each item in the menu.

> **Did You Know?**
>
> *There is no command for hiding and showing the Tools panel.* You cannot hide the Tools panel without hiding the rest of the panels along with it. This is done by choosing Hide Panels under the Window menu or by pressing the Tab key.

Hide All Panels

1. Under the **Window** menu, select **Hide Panels**.

> **TIMESAVER** *Press the Tab key to quickly hide or show all the panels.*

The document window expands to fill the screen.

Expanded Document Window

Resizing the Dock

Located on the right side of your screen is the dock, where the Properties panel and Layers panel are stored by default. If you choose to keep these panels stored, you might occasionally need to expand the dock to focus on specific controls displayed in either panel. This can be especially helpful when working with brushes, gradients, or layers containing lengthy names.

Access the Resize Arrow

1 On the right side of your screen, hover the mouse over the left edge of the dock until a double-sided, horizontal arrow appears.

To expand the dock, click and drag to the left. This creates more room for the panel display and less room for the document window.

To make the dock smaller after you've expanded it, hover over the left edge to access the resize arrow again, and then click and drag to the right.

2 Click and drag the title bar at the top of the docked Layers panel up or down to resize it vertically.

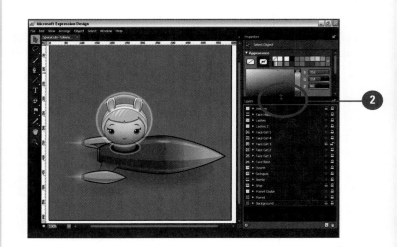

Floating Panels

As you work in Expression Design, you might find that the Properties panel and Layers panel can start to compete with each other for space in the dock. Although you can use the dynamic scroll bar in either panel to access a specific control or layer, it can sometimes be easier to separate the two. When this happens, all you need to do is undock one of the panels and reposition it wherever you'd like, free floating on your screen.

Click the Float Button

1 There is a **Float** button located in the upper right corner of the Properties panel, and also in the Layers panel (but not in the Action bar or Tools panel). Click the **Float** button for each respective panel to remove it from the dock. The panel will then appear free floating on your screen.

2 Click and drag the title bar to reposition the panel wherever you'd like.

Did You Know?

You can also resize floating panels. By clicking and dragging the tab in the bottom right corner of a free-floating panel, you can resize it.

You can create more room vertically in the dock by collapsing Properties panel categories. By clicking the toggle arrow to the right of the category names in the Properties panel, you can collapse each set of controls, making room for the docked Layers panel below it.

Docking Panels

Returning panels to the dock is every bit as easy as removing them. All you need to do is click the Dock button in the upper-right corner of the panel to return it to its previous position within the dock.

Click the Dock Button

1 When a panel is free floating onscreen, the Float button in the upper-right corner becomes a **Dock** button. Click the **Dock** button to return the panel to the dock.

The panel returns to its previous position on the dock.

Did You Know?

The Action bar and Tools panel are permanently docked. You cannot undock them and reposition them free floating on your screen.

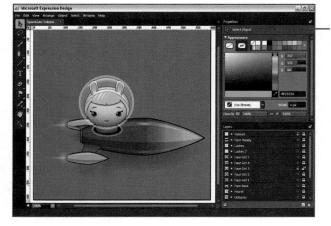

Docked Panel

Showing and Hiding Advanced Properties

The controls in the Properties panel are divided up into categories. You can expand or collapse the category controls from within the panel by clicking the toggle arrow next to each category name. Some categories are hidden until a specific object is selected in the document. For example, the Edit Rectangle category only appears when a rectangle drawn with the Rectangle tool is selected. The only category that is always visible is the Appearance category. At the bottom of this category is a special section containing advanced properties, which are hidden by default. These include settings for applying blend modes, fill rules, and strokes.

Expand or Contract the Appearance Category

① Click the down arrow at the bottom of the **Appearance** category in the **Properties** panel.

The controls displayed in the advanced properties section of the Appearance category change depending on what you currently have selected in the document. Object and Stroke are two of the categories accessible under the advanced properties section of the Properties panel.

Advanced
Controls

Resetting the Active Workspace

After expanding the dock, hiding and showing panels, and repositioning and resizing floating panels onscreen (and vertically in the dock), you might eventually want to get back to basics and return to the default application panel arrangement (known as the Active Workspace). Expression Design contains a special command that allows you to do so instantly.

Choose the Reset Active Workspace Command

1 Under the **Window** menu, choose **Reset Active Workspace**.

The onscreen panel arrangement returns to its original state and appears exactly the way it did when you first launched the application.

> ### Did You Know?
>
> *You cannot save custom workspaces in Expression Design.* With this initial release, you cannot save your favorite onscreen panel arrangements as custom workspaces. Hopefully we will see this feature added in future updates to the application.

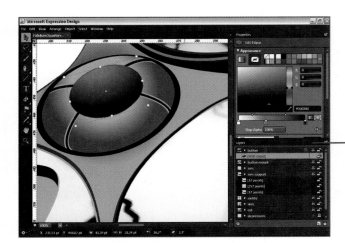

Workspace Is Reset

Selecting Tools

You can access all the tools in Expression Design from the Tools panel, located in the upper-left corner of your screen. Each tool is represented by a descriptive icon. To select a tool, all you need to do is click its icon in the Tools panel. Note that some tools, such as the B-Spline and Polyline tools, are hidden within toolsets, which are accessible from a fly-out list.

Click the Tool Icon

1 From the **Tools** panel, click the icon for the tool that you'd like to work with.

   TIMESAVER *To identify which tool a specific icon represents, hover over it in the Tools panel until a tooltip appears displaying the tool's name.*

2 Icons containing a small white arrow in the bottom-right corner indicate that the tool is part of a set. To access the other tools in the set, click the icon and hold the mouse button down until a fly-out list appears. Point to the tool you'd like to work with and click it.

   The icon for the chosen tool replaces the previously displayed icon in the Tools panel.

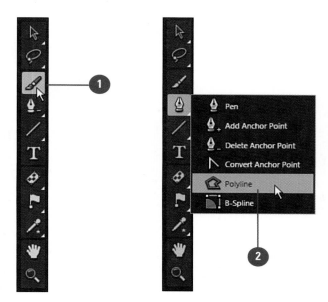

Identifying Tool Shortcuts with Tooltips

Many of the tools in Expression Design are accessible through keyboard shortcuts. Most of the tool shortcuts contain only a single character, which makes them easy to remember; however, should you ever forget one, you can always refer to the tooltip for a reminder.

Refer to the Tooltip

1 Hover over any icon in the **Tools** panel until the tooltip appears displaying the tool's name, followed by the keyboard shortcut in parentheses.

Most tool shortcuts contain only a single character, but some also include the Shift key, such as the Convert Anchor Point tool.

Did You Know?

Keyboard shortcuts are not displayed in the toolset fly-out list. In order to identify the shortcut for a hidden tool, you must refer to the tooltip by hovering over its icon in the fly-out list.

Tooltips are always visible. There is currently no option to disable tooltips in Expression Design.

Some of the tools do not have a keyboard shortcut assigned to them. Certain tools, such as the Polyline, Fill Transform, Start Point, and Reverse Path tools are not accessible with keyboard shortcuts.

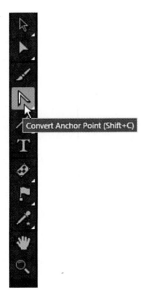

Zooming and Scrolling

3

Introduction

Now that you fully understand how to work with documents and panels in Expression Design, the next step is to master document navigation. So what exactly is navigation, you might ask? Well, when referring to creative software like Expression Design, the term "navigation" is really just a fancy word for zooming and scrolling.

Expression Design's Navigation features allow you to access specifc areas of your document quickly and easily. It's important to develop good navigation skills early on when learning how to use Expression Design because ultimately, they can help you work more efficiently.

There are lots of different ways to zoom and scroll around your documents in Expression Dewsign. In this chapter, you will learn how to apply the various commands for zooming and fitting, as well as how to use the Zoom tool and Pan tool. You will also learn how to center your artwork in the document window, and how to work with multiple views. In addition, you'll learn how to set the mouse wheel options for zooming or scrolling and how to rotate the artboard.

By the end of this chapter, you'll know everything there is to know about document navigation in Expression Design. In the later chapters, you'll use these skills to control the document view and to access specific areas of the artwork quickly and easily.

Navigating with the Zoom Tool

With the Zoom tool, you can increase or decrease the current view magnification for any selected area within a document. There are two ways you can zoom into a specific area with the Zoom tool: by clicking once to zoom incrementally or by clicking and dragging to create a rectangular marquee selection and specify which area of the document you'd like to zoom into.

Click with the Zoom Tool

1. To access the Zoom tool, click the magnifying glass icon in the **Tools** palette.

    TIMESAVER *Press Z to access the Zoom tool quickly.*

    TIMESAVER *Press and hold Ctrl+Spacebar to access the Zoom tool temporarily. Release the keys to return to the previously selected tool.*

2. Hover the cursor over the document area that you'd like to zoom into and then click.

3. Press Alt+click to zoom out.

Marquee with the Zoom Tool

1. To access the Zoom tool, click the magnifying glass icon in the **Tools** palette.

2. Click and drag over the document area that you'd like to zoom into.

3. Alt+click to zoom out.

    TIMESAVER *Press and hold Ctrl+Alt+Spacebar to access the Zoom tool temporarily, then click to zoom out. Release the keys to return to the previously selected tool.*

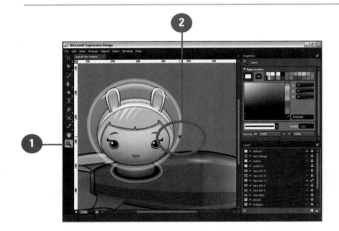

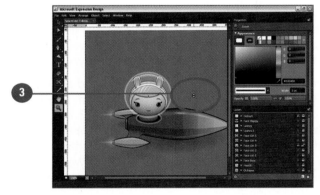

Navigating with the Document Page Zoom Control

Expression Design always displays the current view magnification for the document you are working with in the bottom-left corner of the document window. To change the view magnification, you can enter a custom percentage in the field or choose a preset value from the zoom percentage pop-up list. Note that both these methods apply the zoom using the center of the document as their reference points, regardless of what you might have selected in the document. The reference point cannot be changed.

Choose a Zoom Preset

1. Click the down-facing arrow in the bottom-left corner of the document window (to the right of the current zoom percentage display). A pop-up list of zoom presets appears.

2. Choose a preset zoom percentage from the pop-up list.

   The zoom percentage is instantly applied using the center of the document as a reference point.

Enter a Zoom Percentage

1. The current zoom percentage is displayed in the bottom-left corner of the document window. To change the view, type a new value into the field and press Enter.

   The zoom percentage is instantly applied using the center of the document as a reference point.

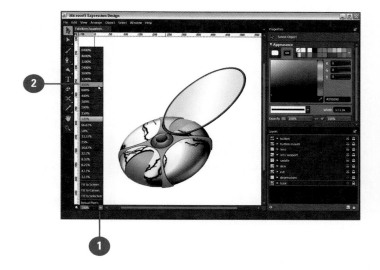

Scrubbing Arrows

> ### Did You Know?
>
> **The current zoom percentage can be adjusted by scrubbing.** Hover over the zoom percentage field in the lower-left corner of the document. When the cursor changes to display a set of four arrows, click and drag up or to the right to increase the value; click and drag down or to the left to decrease.

Navigating with Keyboard Shortcuts

One way to quickly change the current view magnification for a document is to apply the Zoom In and Zoom Out commands. Both of these commands can be accessed under the View menu; however, a much quicker way to apply them is to use keyboard shortcuts.

Click with the Zoom Tool

① Press Ctrl+= to zoom into the center of document. Continue pressing Ctrl+= to zoom in even further. The current view percentage is always displayed in the lower-left corner of the document window.

② Press Ctrl+- to zoom out.

Did You Know?

The Zoom commands always use the center of the document as a reference point. Expression Design does not allow you to change the reference point for the Zoom commands. To zoom into a specific area of the document, you must use the Zoom tool or make a selection and choose Zoom on Selection from the View menu.

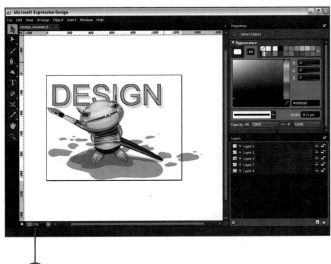

Fitting to Screen

As you work in Expression Design, you might at some point need to see everything you've created, including any items you might have placed in the pasteboard area. The quickest way to fit all your artwork in the document window is to apply the Fit to Screen command.

Apply the Fit to Screen Command

1 To fit all your artwork into the document window—including all items placed in the pasteboard area surrounding the artboard—choose **Fit to Screen** under the **View** menu.

TIMESAVER *Press Ctrl+0 to apply the Fit to Screen command quickly or double-click the Zoom tool icon in the Tools panel.*

All the artwork in the document is displayed in the window.

> ### Did You Know?
>
> ***You can also access the Fit to Screen command from the document window zoom preset list.*** Click the down-facing arrow in the bottom-left corner of the document window (to the right of the current zoom percentage display) to access a pop-up list of zoom presets. Choose Fit to Screen to apply the command.

Artwork Is Fit to Window

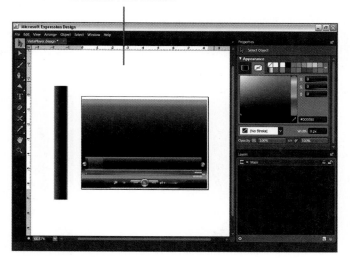

Fitting to Canvas

The best way to preview your artwork onscreen is to display the entire artboard in the document window. The Fit to Screen command works well for this purpose, but only if no items are placed in the surrounding pasteboard area. This is because Fit to Screen will display everything in the document, including items on the pasteboard. To display the artboard without any surrounding pasteboard objects, you must apply the Fit to Canvas command.

Apply the Fit to Canvas Command

1 Click the down-facing arrow in the bottom-left corner of the document window (to the right of the current zoom percentage display). A pop-up list of zoom presets appears.

2 To fit the entire artboard in the document window (not including any items placed in the surrounding pasteboard area), choose **Fit to Canvas** from the pop-up list.

The entire artboard is displayed in the window.

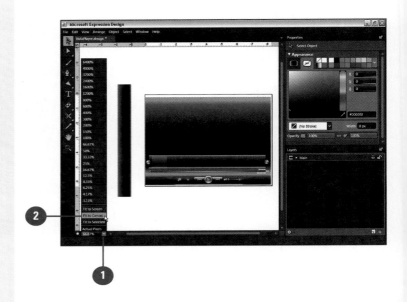

Artboard Is Fit to Window

Fitting to Selected

No matter what objects you have selected, Expression Design always uses the center of the document as the reference point when zooming with the Zoom In or Zoom Out commands, or when choosing one of the preset zoom percentages from the document window preset list. To zoom in on a selected object, you can use the Zoom tool or, to zoom even more precisely, apply the Fit to Selected or Zoom on Selection commands.

Apply the Fit to Selected Command

1 Select the item(s) you'd like to magnify with either the Selection tool or Direct Selection tool. Shift+click to select multiple items.

2 Click the down-facing arrow in the bottom-left corner of the document window (to the right of the current zoom percentage display). A pop-up list of zoom presets appears.

3 To fit the selected object(s) in the document window, choose **Fit to Selected** from the pop-up list.

The selected object is magnified to fit in the window.

Apply the Zoom on Selection Command

1 Select the item(s) you'd like to magnify with either the Selection tool or Direct Selection tool. Shift+click to select multiple items.

2 Under the **View** menu, choose **Zoom on Selection**.

The selected object is magnified to fit in the window.

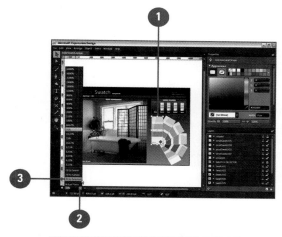

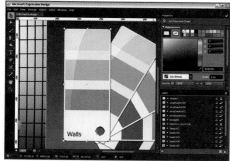

Viewing Actual Size

Viewing artwork at its actual size means displaying it onscreen at 100% view magnification. When you view artwork at its actual size, what you are seeing is the piece displayed at the exact width and height dimensions that will print or export.

Apply the Actual Size Command

1 To display your artwork in the document window at a view magnification of 100%, choose **Actual Size** from the **View** menu.

> **TIMESAVER** *Press Ctrl+1 to apply the Actual Size command quickly.*

> **TIMESAVER** *Double-click the Pan tool in the Tools panel to view the art at actual size.*

The artwork is displayed at 100%.

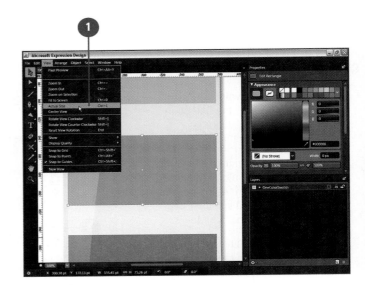

Did You Know?

The Actual Size command does not center your view. By applying the Actual Size command, you are telling Expression Design to change the view magnification to 100%—not to center the artboard in the document window. To center the artboard, you must apply the Center View command.

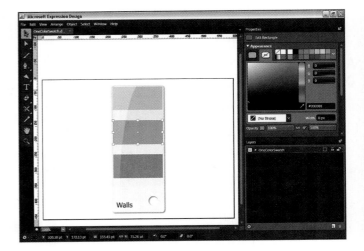

Centering View

The Center View command allows you to center the artboard in the document window at 100% view magnification. Applying this command is the quickest and easiest way to return to centered view after navigating around the document with the Zoom and Pan tools.

Apply the Center View Command

1 To center your artwork in the document window, choose **Center View** from the **View** menu.

The artboard is centered and displayed at 100% in the window.

Did You Know?

Applying the Center View command also changes the document view magnification to 100%. By applying the Center View command, you are not only telling Expression Design to center the artboard in the document window but also to change the current view magnification to 100%.

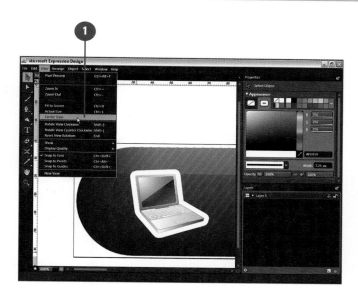

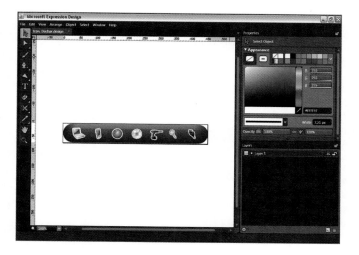

Working with Multiple Views

The New View command allows you to create multiple document windows for the same open document. By doing so, you can view your artwork at different zoom percentages. With New View, you can create one window for zoomed-in detail work and a separate one for previewing the entire artboard. In fact, you can create as many views as you like.

Apply the New View Command

1 To create a second window for the currently active document, choose **New View** from the **View** menu.

2 In the new window that appears, use any of the methods described in this chapter to apply a different view percentage.

3 Toggle between views by

◆ Choosing the document name from the **Window** menu (multiple views are numbered)

◆ Clicking the document name in the Flip bar

◆ Choosing the document from the Flip bar active files menu (multiple views are numbered)

4 To close an individual view for a document, click the Close button displayed next to the document name in the Flip bar. To close all views at once, choose **Close** from the **File** menu.

> ### Did You Know?
>
> *Changes made to the artwork are reflected in every view of the document.* Edits made to the artwork when working with multiple views are reflected in every view of the document.

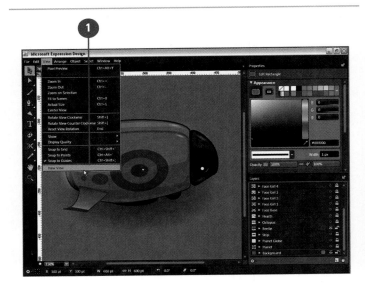

Close Button

Scrolling with Scroll Bars

Another way that you can navigate around the document is by using the document window scroll bars. When you zoom in on your artwork, say to 300% view magnification, the document window can no longer fit the entire artboard in its display area. Rather than zoom out to access another part of the document, you can instead use the scroll bars to reposition the artboard in the window.

Click and Drag the Scroll Bars

1 To access the document window's vertical and horizontal scroll bars, use any of the methods described in this chapter for zooming into the document.

2 Click and drag the scroll bars to reposition the artwork in the window.

Did You Know?

The pasteboard area surrounding the artboard is infinite. If you click and drag the scroll bars in either direction until they reach the edge of the window, Expression Design automatically adds more pasteboard area, thereby making it infinitely scrollable.

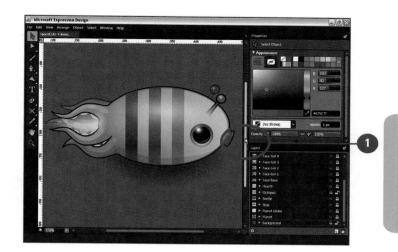

Scrolling with the Pan Tool

The Pan tool offers a much more free-form method for scrolling around the document. If you need to access a specific area of the document quickly, don't waste time by applying multiple zoom commands or dragging the scroll bars. Instead, access the Pan tool and click and drag in any direction. Clicking with the Pan tool causes the cursor's icon to grab the artboard; dragging repositions the artboard in the window.

Click and Drag with the Pan Tool

① To access the Pan tool, click the hand icon in the Tools panel.

TIMESAVER *Press H to access the Pan tool quickly.*

TIMESAVER *Press and hold the Spacebar to access the Pan tool temporarily. Release the Spacebar to return to the previously selected tool.*

② Click and drag with the Pan tool to reposition the artwork in the window.

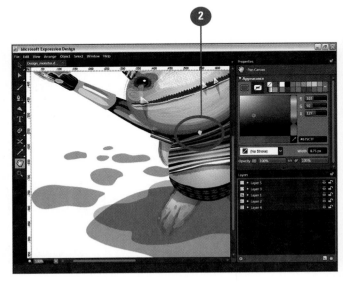

Zooming with the Mouse Wheel

Expression Design also includes an option for zooming with the mouse wheel. With this option enabled, you can zoom in and out of the document without having to access the Zoom tool or apply any of the Zoom commands. There's also an option that allows the position of the mouse to determine the reference point for zooming.

Changing Mouse Wheel Options

1 Under the **Edit** menu, point to **Options** and choose **General**.

> **TIMESAVER** *Press Ctrl+K to quickly access the General pane of the Options dialog box.*

2 In the Options dialog box that appears, choose **Zoom** from the **Mouse Wheel Usage** drop-down list.

3 Check the **Mouse Wheel Zoom About Mouse Position** option to allow the position of the mouse to determine the reference point for zooming.

4 Click **OK** to apply the mouse wheel zoom options.

5 Scroll the mouse wheel up to zoom in; scroll down to zoom out. Zoom percentages are applied incrementally in the document with each position of the mouse wheel.

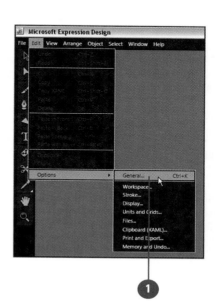

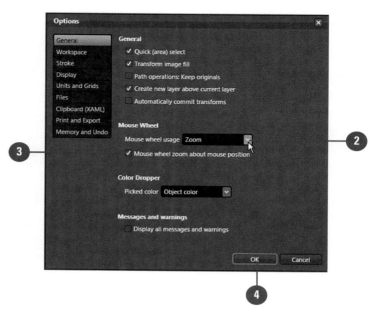

Scrolling with the Mouse Wheel

If you prefer, you can set the mouse wheel option in Expression Design for scrolling rather than zooming. This option is somewhat limited in that it only allows you to use the mouse wheel to scroll vertically or horizontally, but not both.

Changing Mouse Wheel Options

1. Under the **Edit** menu, point to **Options** and choose **General**.

   TIMESAVER *Press Ctrl+K to quickly access the General pane of the Options dialog box.*

2. In the Options dialog box that appears, choose **Vertical Scrolling** or **Horizontal Scrolling** from the **Mouse Wheel Usage** drop-down list.

   IMPORTANT *Although it does not appear grayed out, the Mouse Wheel Zoom About Mouse Position option has no effect when Mouse Wheel Usage is set for scrolling.*

3. Click **OK** to apply the mouse wheel zoom options.

4. Scroll the mouse wheel up or down to reposition the artwork in the window.

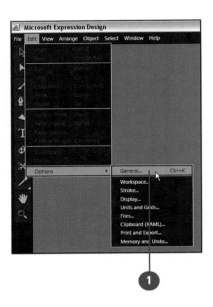

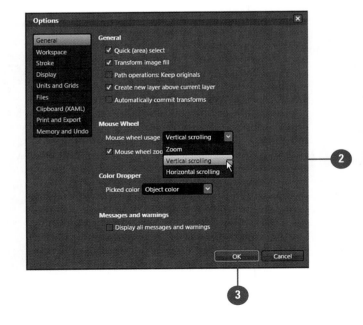

Rotating the Artboard ▶

One of the nicer features in Expression Design is the ability to rotate the artboard. This can be especially useful when drawing freehand or applying shading or cross hatch with the simulated natural media brushes. It's nice to be able to rotate your artboard onscreen just as if it were a piece of drawing paper.

Apply the Rotate Commands

① Under the **View** menu, choose **Rotate View Clockwise** or **Rotate View Counter Clockwise.**

TIMESAVER *Press Shift+[to apply the Rotate View Clockwise command; press Shift+] to apply Rotate View Counter Clockwise.*

② The artboard appears rotated in the window. To rotate the artboard even further, continue applying the rotate commands.

③ To return the artboard back to its original position, choose **Reset View Rotation** from the **View** menu.

TIMESAVER *Press the End key to apply the Reset View Rotation command quickly.*

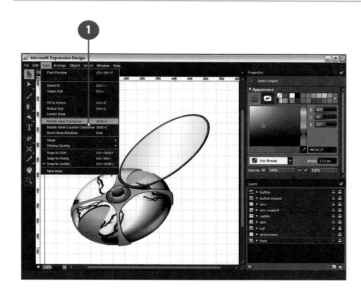

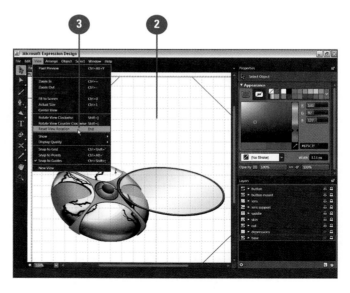

Did You Know?

Ruler units disappear when applying the Rotate View commands. Rotating the artboard causes the rulers to appear blank.

Ruler guides rotate with the artboard, but the document grid does not. Existing ruler guides rotate along with the artboard, but the document grid always remains static.

Working with Grids, Guides, and Points

Introduction

Any good design application includes options for aligning objects to the document grid and to ruler guides. Expression Design is no exception; however, it does up the ante a bit with its Snap to Points feature, which allows you to align objects based on the position of each object's bounding box nodes.

In this chapter, you'll learn everything there is to know about working with grids, guides, and points in Expression Design. The lessons teach you how to show and hide grids and guides as you work and how to snap objects in place using the guide, grid, and point snap features. You will also learn how to change the size of the document grid and how to reposition and remove ruler guides.

This chapter also introduces you to working with ruler guides on a rotated canvas—a unique feature in Expression Design that allows you to create angled guides. In addition, you will learn how to create guides based on existing shapes and paths and how to revert them back to editable objects.

After you start working with grids, guides, and points in Expression Design, you'll come to rely on them for aligning objects precisely and creating balanced designs. You'll put these skills to use right away as you begin working with objects in later chapters.

Showing and Hiding the Grid

The document grid serves as a useful tool for aligning objects precisely in your artwork. You can snap objects to the grid as you create and transform them or use the grid as a visual guide to line objects up evenly. However, to use the grid as a reference guide for precise object positioning, you must first learn how to control its visibility in the document.

Choose the Show Grid Command

① To display the document grid, choose **Show** from the **View** menu and point to **Grid**. Whenever you make the grid visible, Expression Design displays a check mark next to the word Grid in the submenu.

TIMESAVER *Press Ctrl+' to toggle visibility for the document grid.*

② To hide the document grid, choose **Grid** from the **Show** submenu again or apply the keyboard shortcut Ctrl+'.

Did You Know?

The Show Grid command only affects the currently active document. When multiple documents are open, the Show Grid command only toggles grid visibility for the document you are currently working in.

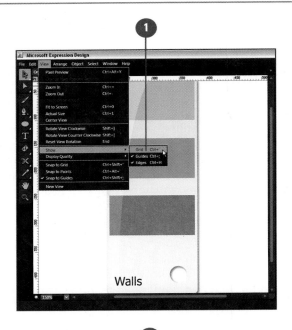

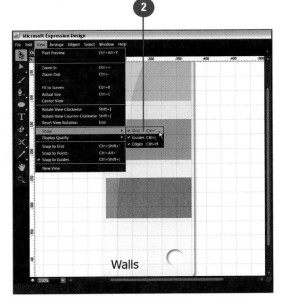

Changing Grid Size

Changing Grid Size Options

1 Under the **Edit** menu, point to **Options** and choose **Units and Grids.**

> **TIMESAVER** *Press Ctrl+K to quickly access the Options dialog box. Select Units and Grids from the menu on the left.*

2 In the Units and Grids pane of the Options dialog box, double-click the current value in the **Grid Size** field and enter a different size. The value you enter determines the size of each square in the grid.

3 Click **OK** to apply the new grid size.

Did You Know?

The Grid Size option uses the same measurement unit as the Document Units option. In the Units and Grids pane of the Options dialog box, the measurement unit that you choose in the Document Units field determines what measurement unit is displayed in the neighboring Grid Size field.

Grid size options are accessible via the Units and Grids pane of the Options dialog box. This setting determines the size of each square in the document grid, allowing you to customize the overall size of the grid to meet the alignment needs of your project.

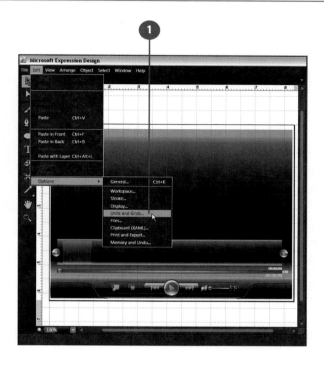

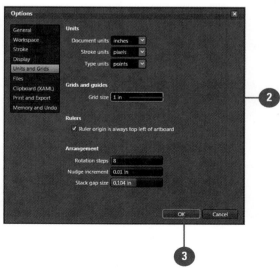

Using the Grid as a Drawing Guide

As you draw shapes and paths in Expression Design, you can refer to the document grid to ensure that certain objects are aligned evenly, such as custom interface controls or website navigation buttons. After the objects are aligned, you can always toggle the grid's visibility on or off, should the overlying pattern become too distracting to work with.

Align to the Grid as You Draw

1. To display the document grid, choose **Show** from the **View** menu and point to **Grid**. Whenever you make the grid visible, Expression Design displays a check mark next to the word Grid in the submenu.

   TIMESAVER *Press Ctrl+' to toggle visibility for the document grid.*

2. As you create shapes and paths using the various drawing tools, you can use the document grid to align their positions on the artboard.

3. To preview your artwork without displaying the overlying document grid, choose **Grid** from the **Show** submenu, or apply the keyboard shortcut of Ctrl+'.

See Also

See Chapter 8, "Drawing Shapes and Paths" to learn more about working with the various drawing tools in Expression Design.

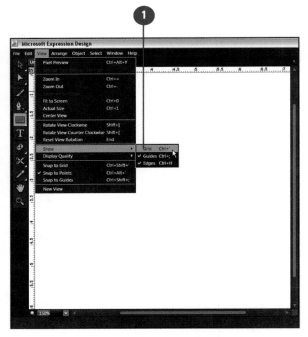

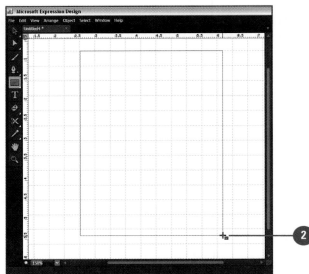

Snapping to the Grid When Drawing

An even more precise way to align objects as you draw them is to snap to the document grid. This technique allows you to align the position of each line, point, or shape precisely on the artboard as you use the various drawing tools in Expression Design.

Enable the Snap to Grid Option

① To display the document grid, choose **Show** from the **View** menu and point to **Grid**. Then, under the **View** menu, choose **Snap to Grid**. Expression Design displays a check mark next to the menu command whenever it is enabled.

TIMESAVER *Press Ctrl+' to toggle visibility for the document grid.*

TIMESAVER *Press Ctrl+Shift+' to toggle the Snap to Grid command on and off.*

② If you click or drag close enough to any gridline with the various drawing tools (such as the Pen or Rectangle), the individual points (or lines) snap into position. Snapping to the grid allows you to align the position of each line, point, or shape precisely on the artboard.

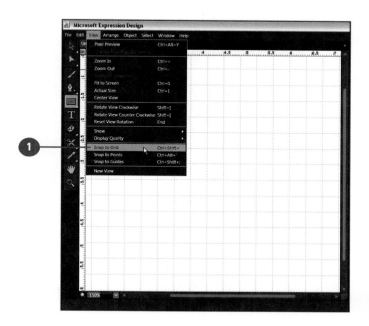

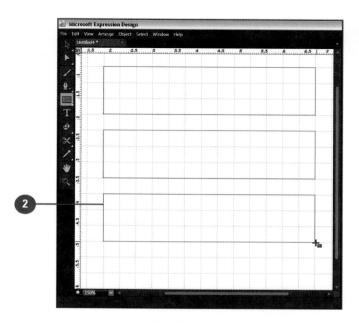

Snapping to the Grid When Moving Objects

You might find it easier to align objects to the document grid after they've been drawn. One of the benefits to working this way is that you can snap objects to the grid while it is hidden, thereby eliminating the need to display the checkerboard overlay pattern. When guide snaps are enabled, you can move objects on the artboard and refer to the intersection markers that are displayed over any bounding box points that intersect with the grid.

Enable the Snap to Grid Option

1. To display the document grid, choose **Show** from the **View** menu and point to **Grid**. Then, under the **View** menu, choose **Snap to Grid**. Expression Design displays a check mark next to the menu command whenever it is enabled.

   TIMESAVER *Press Ctrl+' to toggle visibility for the document grid.*

   TIMESAVER *Press Ctrl+Shift+' to toggle the Snap to Grid command on and off.*

2. Press V to access the Selection tool and click and drag an object in any direction to reposition it. When you drag close enough to a gridline, the object automatically snaps into position.

3. As you click and drag, Expression Design displays red intersection markers over any points that come in contact with the grid.

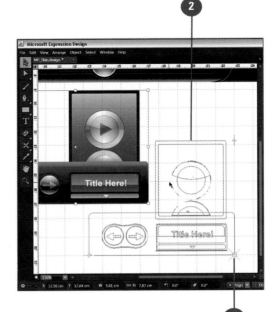

Adding Ruler Guides

When it comes to aligning objects, some designers prefer to use ruler guides as opposed to the document grid. This is because ruler guides can be positioned wherever you like on the artboard, whereas the document grid's position is limited to the settings assigned in the Units and Grids pane of the Options dialog box.

Drag from the Rulers

1 Hover over the ruler area and click and hold down the mouse button. The cursor changes to display a double-sided arrow.

2 Drag a guide out from the ruler area onto the artboard.

3 When the guide is positioned where you like, release the mouse button.

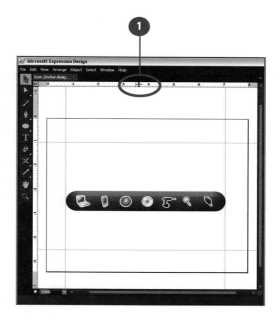

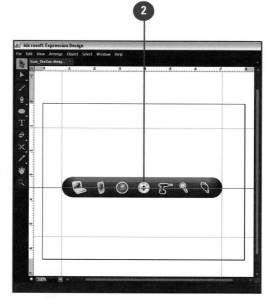

Did You Know?

Ruler guides always extend past the edges of the artboard. All ruler guides extend into the pasteboard area surrounding the artboard.

Ruler guides automatically rotate with the artboard. Unlike the document grid, if you rotate the artboard using the Rotate View commands, the ruler guides also rotate.

Ruler guides are not layer specific. Unlike objects, ruler guides are not positioned within a layer; therefore, they are not affected by assigned layer color or the Layers panel visibility controls.

Ruler guides are not printable. The ruler guides can only be viewed onscreen as you work in Expression Design. They will not print or export with the artwork.

Showing and Hiding Guides

The more guides you add to your document, the more distracting they can become. That's why the best way to work with ruler guides is to display them onscreen only when you need them. Thankfully, Expression Design makes it easy to control guide visibility through the use of menu commands, keyboard shortcuts, and contextual menus.

Choose the Show Guides Command

1 To display ruler guides, choose **Show** from the **View** menu and point to **Guides**. Whenever you make the guides visible, Expression Design displays a check mark next to the word **Guides** in the submenu.

TIMESAVER *Press Ctrl+; to toggle visibility for ruler guides.*

2 To hide the ruler guides, choose **Guides** from the **Show** submenu again or apply the keyboard shortcut Ctrl+;.

> ### Did You Know?
>
> **You can also access the Show Guides command from the contextual menu.** To access the Show Guides command from the contextual menu, make sure you have no objects selected, and then right-click anywhere in the document and choose Show Guides.

Snapping to Guides

Snapping objects to ruler guides allows you to align objects precisely on the artboard. The benefit to snapping to ruler guides as opposed to the grid is that you can place guides and reposition them wherever you like on the artboard—even at an angle—whereas the document grid always remains static.

Enable the Snap to Guides Option

① To display the ruler guides, choose **Show** from the **View** menu and point to **Guides**.

> **TIMESAVER** *Press Ctrl+; to toggle visibility for ruler guides.*

② Under the **View** menu, choose **Snap to Guides**.

> **TIMESAVER** *Press Ctrl+Shift+; to toggle the Snap to Guides command on and off.*

③ Press **V** to access the Selection tool and click and drag an object in any direction. When you drag close enough to a guide, the object automatically snaps to it.

Did You Know?

The ruler guides change color when guide snaps are enabled. When the Snap to Guides option is enabled, the ruler guides appear blue; when the option is disabled, the guides appear gray.

Intersection markers are displayed when snapping to guides. Expression Design displays intersection markers over any bounding box points that come in contact with the ruler guides. However, unlike the document grid, the guides must be visible for the intersection markers to appear.

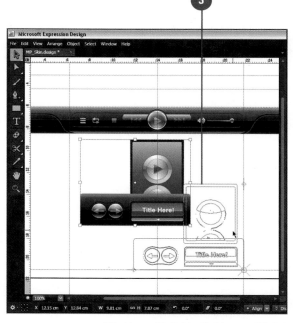

Repositioning Guides

Once you drag a ruler guide onto the artboard and release the mouse button, it remains in place and cannot be selected or moved with any of the selection tools. Expression Design purposely locks the guides to prevent you from accidentally selecting and moving them as you transform objects in your artwork. However, it is possible to reposition guides. To do so, you must hold down the Alt key while you click and drag the guide.

Alt+Click and Drag

1 Hover the mouse cursor over the ruler guide that you'd like to reposition on the artboard.

2 Hold down the **Alt** key and click and drag to the left or right (for vertical guides) or up or down (for horizontal guides).

3 When the guide is positioned where you like, release the mouse button.

Did You Know?

You do not have to access a specific tool in order to reposition the ruler guides. You can always reposition the guides by Alt+clicking and dragging, no matter what tool you have selected in the Tool panel.

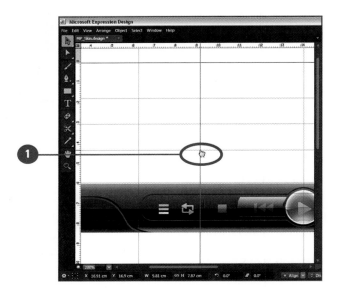

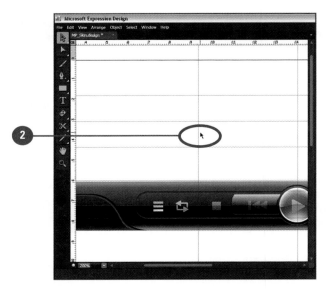

Removing Guides

Ruler guides can be removed from a document just as easily as they can be added. All you need to do is Alt+click while you drag each guide back into the respective horizontal or vertical ruler area where you originally pulled them from.

Alt+Click and Drag to the Rulers

1 Hover the mouse cursor over the ruler guide that you'd like to remove from the artboard.

2 Hold down the **Alt** key and click and drag the guide back into the ruler area on the far left of the document window (for vertical guides) or up into the ruler area at the top of the document window (for horizontal guides).

3 Release the mouse button.

Did You Know?

You can only move or delete one guide at a time. Expression Design does not allow you to select and move multiple guides at once. There is also currently no command for clearing all ruler guides from the document.

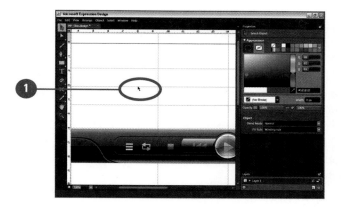

Creating Angled Guides

When applying either of the Rotate View commands, any existing ruler guides that you've added to the document rotate along with the artboard. In addition, any new guides that you add while the artboard is rotated are not angled to match the existing guides. This curious behavior allows you to create angled guides that can be used to align objects after the artboard is returned to its original position.

Add Guides and Rotate the View

1. Add some ruler guides to the artboard by clicking and dragging from the horizontal or vertical rulers.

2. Under the **View** menu, choose **Rotate View Clockwise** or **Rotate View Counter Clockwise.**

   TIMESAVER *Press Shift+[to apply the Rotate View Clockwise command; press Shift+] to apply Rotate View Counter Clockwise.*

3. The artboard, including the ruler guides, now appears rotated in the document window. To rotate the artboard even further, continue applying the rotate commands.

4. Add some more ruler guides to the artboard by clicking and dragging from the horizontal or vertical rulers. These new guides do not appear rotated.

5. Return the artboard back to its original position by choosing **Reset View Rotation** from the **View** menu.

   TIMESAVER *Press the End key to apply the Reset View Rotation command quickly.*

   The second set of guides that you added now appears angled.

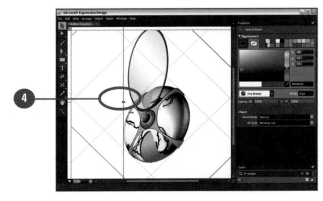

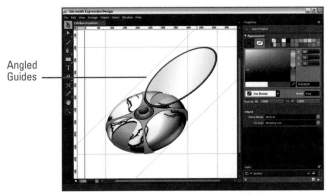

Angled Guides

Making and Releasing Guides

Expression Design also allows you to convert existing shapes or paths into guides. These types of guides can be used to indicate specific areas of a design where certain objects, such as text, should be positioned. You can also revert these guides back into editable shapes once the guides are no longer needed.

Apply the Guide Commands

1 Use the various drawing tools, such as the Pen or Rectangle, to create a shape or path. After it is drawn, be sure not to deselect it.

2 To make a guide out of the selected shape or path, choose **Guide** from the **Object** menu and choose **Make**.

> **TIMESAVER** *Press Ctrl+5 to apply the Make command quickly.*

3 To revert the made guide back into an editable shape or path, choose **Guide** from the **Object** menu and point to **Release**.

> **IMPORTANT** *Guides created from shapes or paths cannot be repositioned. You cannot Alt+click and drag a guide created from a shape or path.*

Did You Know?

The Release command reverts all made guides back into editable shapes. It is currently not possible to select and release individual guides created from shapes or paths.

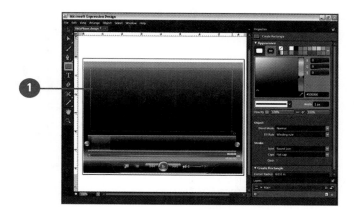

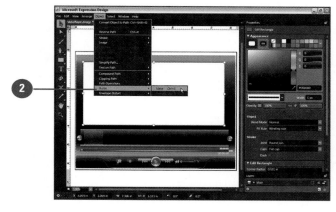

Snapping to Points

In addition to aligning objects to the document grid and to ruler guides, you can also align objects to each other using the Snap to Points feature. When you enable this option, any objects that you move around on the artboard automatically snap to the bounding box nodes of a neighboring shape or path.

Enable the Snap to Points Option

① Use the various drawing tools, such as the Pen or Rectangle, to create some shapes and/or paths.

② Under the **View** menu, choose **Snap to Points**. Expression Design displays a check mark next to the menu command whenever it is enabled.

TIMESAVER *Press Ctrl+Alt+' to toggle the Snap to Points command on and off.*

③ Press **V** to access the Selection tool and click and drag one of the shapes or paths in any direction. When you drag close enough to one of the bounding box selection points for a neighboring object (not the points that make up the path), the object automatically snaps to it.

④ As you click and drag, Expression Design displays red intersection markers over any points that come in contact with the grid.

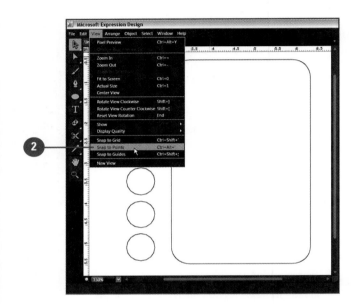

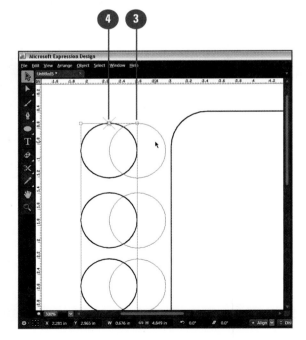

Making Selections

Introduction

The first step when learning how to work with objects (which include shapes, paths, text, and imported graphics) is to understand how to select them in the document. To move, transform, apply attributes, or edit objects in any way, you have to select them first.

In this chapter, you'll use the various selection-making tools that are available in Expression Design. This includes the Selection tool, the Direct Selection tool, the Lasso Selection tool, and the Group Select tool. You'll learn how to select individual objects, how to select multiple objects, how to select objects from within a group, and how to select the paths and points that define a shape. You'll also learn how to select multiple objects or points on a path by drawing a rectangular or free-form marquee with the different selection-making tools.

With Expression Design, you can also make selections by applying commands rather than using tools. The Select All command allows you to select every object in the document at once, and the Select By command allows you to select objects containing similar attributes, such as fill color or stroke color.

After you've mastered how to make good selections, you'll be well on your way to learning how to work with objects effectively.

What You'll Do

Select with the Selection Tool

Select with the Direct Selection Tool

Make a Marquee Selection

Select with the Lasso Tool

Select with the Group Select Tool

Select All

Select By

Deselect

Selecting with the Selection Tool

You can use the Selection tool to select individual or multiple objects in a document and move or transform them. After you select the object, Expression Design displays a bounding box around it. You can select and move the bounding box nodes to change an object's shape and to scale editable text objects and imported graphics.

Select Individual Objects

① Access the Selection tool by clicking its icon (the black arrow) at the top of the **Tools** panel.

IMPORTANT *If the black arrow icon is not visible at the top of the Tools panel, it is hidden behind the Group Selection tool. Click the Group Selection tool icon and hold the mouse button down to access the Selection tool from the fly-out menu.*

TIMESAVER *Press V to access the Selection tool quickly.*

② Click directly on the path of any object to select it.

③ If the object contains a fill color (other than None), you can also select it by clicking on the fill area of the shape. Expression Design displays a bounding box around the object after it is selected.

Did You Know?

You can also select text objects with the Selection tool. To select a text object with the Selection tool, click on any character.

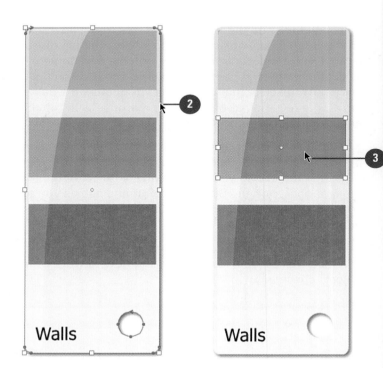

Select Multiple Objects

1 Access the Selection tool by clicking its icon (the black arrow) at the top of the **Tools** panel.

2 To select multiple objects, hold down **Shift** as you click with the Selection tool.

Did You Know?

When multiple objects are selected, their paths are revealed. When more than one object is selected at a time, Expression Design displays a colored outline around each shape and reveals all the points that make up each path. The color of each selected object's outline is determined by which layer the object is on. If the outline color is the same for all selected objects, they currently all reside on the same layer.

See Also

See Chapter 7, "Working with Layers," to learn more about working with layered objects in Expression Design.

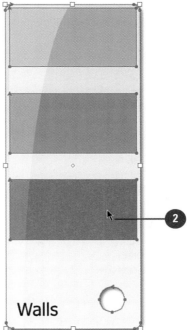

Walls

Selecting with the Direct Selection Tool

You can use the Direct Selection tool to select, move, or delete path segments or individual points along a path. Doing so allows you to edit the shape of an object. You can also use the Direct Selection tool to select an object's entire path and reposition it on the artboard or to select individual objects within a group.

Select Path Segments

1. Access the Direct Selection tool by clicking its icon (the white arrow tip) in the **Tools** panel.

   IMPORTANT *If the white arrow tip icon is not visible in the Tools panel, it is hidden behind the Lasso Selection tool. Click the Lasso Selection tool icon and hold the mouse button down to access the Direct Selection tool from the fly-out menu.*

   TIMESAVER *Press A to access the Selection tool quickly.*

2. Click directly on a path segment of any object to select it. Expression Design displays a colored outline around the object when the path segment is selected. The outline color is determined by which layer the object currently resides on.

   Expression Design also displays a small blue square at the exact point where you clicked along the path.

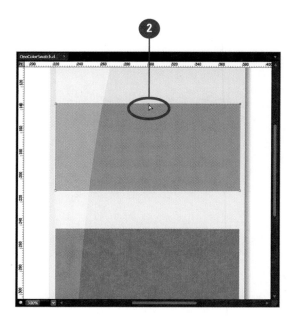

Select Individual Points

1 Access the Direct Selection tool by clicking its icon (the white arrow tip) in the **Tools** panel.

2 Click directly on a path segment of any object to select it. All the points that make up the path are made visible by clicking with the Direct Selection tool. By clicking and moving these points with the Direct Selection tool, you can edit the shape. When selected, the points appear filled in; when deselected, they appear hollow. Shift+click or marquee to select multiple points.

When hovering over a point along a path, Expression Design displays a point icon under the cursor. You can use this icon to locate points without having to click on a path segment to reveal them.

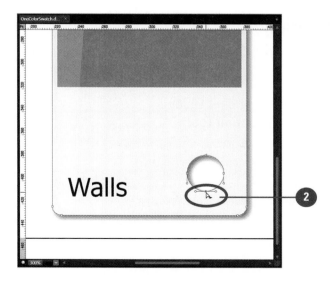

Did You Know?

You can also select an entire path with the Direct Selection tool. If the object contains a fill color (other than None), you can select the entire path (all segements) by clicking on the fill area of the shape with the Direct Selection Tool. When the entire path is selected, all the points along the path appear filled in.

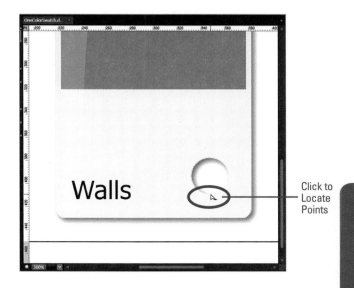

Click to Locate Points

Making a Marquee Selection

Another great way to select multiple objects at once (besides Shift+clicking) is to draw a rectangular marquee over them with the Selection tool. You can also use this techinque with the Direct Selection tool to select multiple points along a path (or paths).

Click and Drag over Objects with the Selection Tool

1. Access the Selection tool by clicking its icon (the black arrow) at the top of the **Tools** panel.

2. Use the Selection tool to click and drag a marquee around the object (or multiple objects) that you'd like to select.

   After you complete your selection, Expression Design displays a bounding box around the object(s).

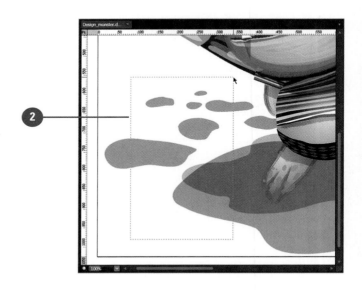

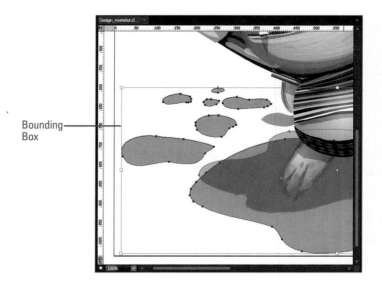

Bounding Box

Click and Drag over Points with the Direct Selection Tool

① Access the Direct Selection tool by clicking its icon (the white arrow tip) in the **Tools** panel.

② With the Direct Selection tool, you can click and drag over specific points along a path (or paths) to select them.

IMPORTANT *If you marquee with the Direct Selection tool over an area of a path segment that does not contain any points, then the entire path is selected.*

After the points (or the entire path) are selected, Expression Design displays an outline around the object's path using the currently assigned layer color. Selected points appear filled in with the same color.

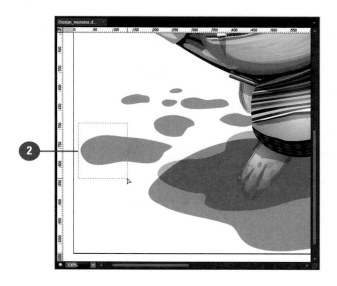

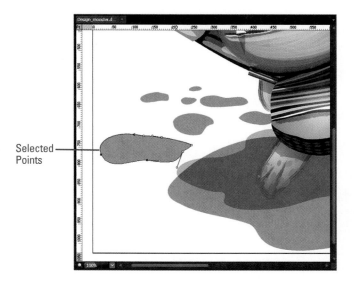

Selected Points

Selecting with the Lasso Tool

▶

Working with a rectangular marquee can sometimes cause you to select more objects or points than you would like, especially when editing a detailed design that contains a lot of shapes. A better way to select objects or points in a complicated design is to draw over them with the Lasso Selection tool, which allows you to make free-form selections.

Click and Drag to Create a Free-Form Selection

1 Access the Lasso Selection tool by clicking its icon in the **Tools** panel.

> **IMPORTANT** *If the lasso icon is not visible in the Tools panel, it is hidden behind the Direct Selection tool. Click the Direct Selection tool icon and hold the mouse button down to access the Lasso Selection tool from the fly-out menu.*

> **TIMESAVER** *Press Q to access the Selection tool quickly.*

2 When hovering over a point along a path, Expression Design displays a point icon under the cursor. You can use this icon to locate points without having to click on a path segment to reveal them. Click directly on a point (or path segment) of any object to select it.

3 To create a free-form lasso selection, click and drag over specific points along the path.

> **IMPORTANT** *If you marquee over an area of a path segment that does not contain any points, the entire path is selected.*

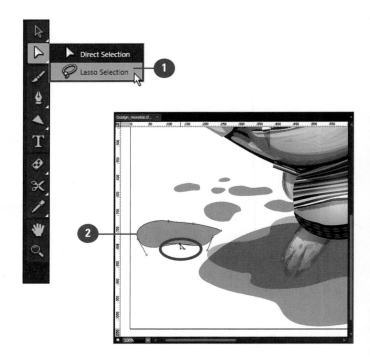

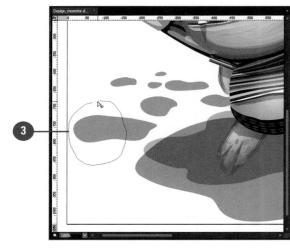

Selecting with the Group Select Tool

Grouping objects together allows you to move and transform them collectively, rather than one by one. Although this can be a huge timesaver, it can also make it difficult to select and edit a single object from within the group. Rather than ungrouping to select and edit a single member of the group, it's much more efficient to select it using the Group Select tool. Doing so allows you to select and edit the object from within the group, without having to apply the Ungroup command first.

Select Objects Within a Group

1. To create a grouped object, select multiple objects and choose **Group** under the **Arrange** menu. The objects can now be moved and transformed collectively.

   TIMESAVER *Press Ctrl+G to apply the Group command quickly.*

2. Access the Group Select tool by clicking its icon in the **Tools** panel.

   IMPORTANT *If the Group Select icon is not visible in the Tools panel, it is hidden behind the Selection tool. Click the Selection tool icon and hold the mouse button down to access the Group Select tool from the fly-out menu.*

   TIMESAVER *Press Shift+A to access the Group Select tool quickly.*

3. Click directly on the path of any object within the group to select it. If the object contains a fill color (other than None), you can also select it by clicking on the fill area of the shape. Expression Design displays a bounding box around the object after it is selected.

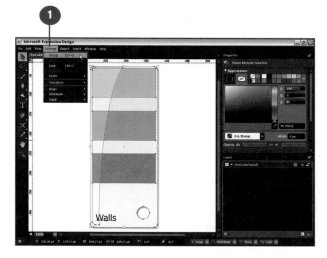

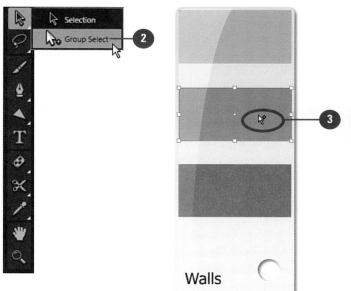

Selecting All

There are a couple of different ways that you can select every object in the document. One way is to draw a marquee over all the objects using the Selection tool, or you could use a much better technique, which is to apply the Select All command. Doing so is not only a lot quicker, but also more accurate.

Apply the Select All Command

1 Under the **Select** menu, choose **All**.

> **TIMESAVER** *Press Ctrl+A to apply the Select All command quickly.*

All objects in the document (that are not locked) are automatically selected. As always, Expression Design displays a bounding box around the selected objects.

Did You Know?

Locked objects cannot be selected. Any objects that have been locked using the lock controls in the Layers panel or by applying the Lock command cannot be selected with any of the selection tools or by applying any of the Select commands.

See Also

See Chapter 6, "Working with Objects," to learn more about locking and grouping objects in Expression Design.

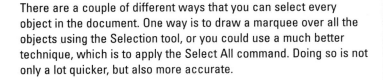

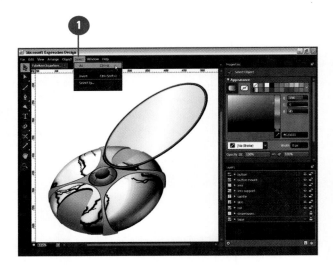

All Unlocked Objects Are Selected

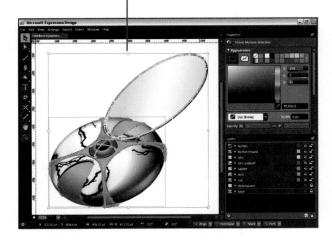

Selecting By

Expression Design also contains a special feature that allows you to make selections based on certain applied attributes, such as fill color, stroke color, and brush stroke. The Select By dialog box also contains an option for selecting text objects that use the same font. You can use this feature to select similar items in a document and edit them all at once.

Select Multiple Objects Based on Specific Attributes

① Select any item in the document to use as a source object. Under the **Select** menu, choose **Select By**.

② In the Select By dialog box that appears, choose which attributes the objects should have in common with the source object. Options include Stroke Name (for selecting objects with the same brush stroke applied), Stroke Color, Fill, and Font (for selecting editable text objects with the same font applied).

③ Clilck **OK** to apply the Select By command. Expression Design automatically selects all objects in the document that meet the parameters chosen in the Select By dialog box.

Did You Know?

The Select By command recognizes None fills. If the source object has a None fill, the Select By command is able to locate and select other objects with a None fill. However, it cannot locate and select other objects with no stroke applied.

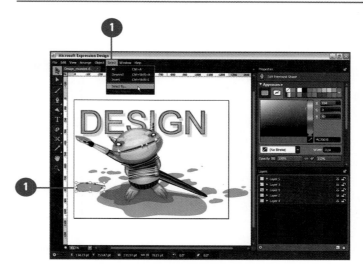

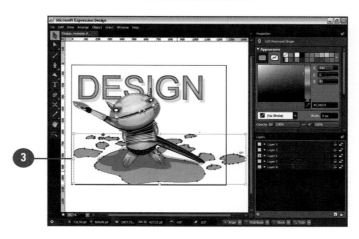

Deselecting

When you are finished working with a selected object (or multiple selected objects), you should always deselect before moving on to the next task. You can deselect objects in Expression Design in one of two ways: by applying the Deselect command or by clicking in any blank area of the document with one of the selection-making tools.

Apply the Deselect Command

1 Select an object (or objects) using any of the selection methods described throughout this chapter.

2 Under the **Select** menu, choose **Deselect**.

> **TIMESAVER** *Press Ctrl+Shift+A to apply the Deselect command quickly.*

All objects that were previously selected in the document are automatically deselected, and the selection bounding box disappears.

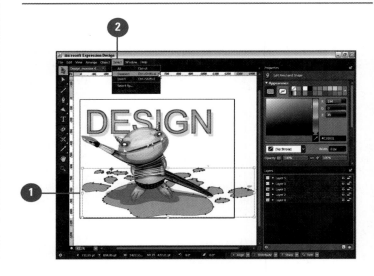

All Objects Are Deselected

Click in Any Blank Area of the Document

① Select an object (or objects) using any of the selection methods described throughout this chapter.

② Access any of the selection tools (Selection, Direct Selection, Lasso Selection, or Group Select) by clicking its icon in the **Tools** panel.

③ Click in any blank area of the document (on the artboard or off) to deselect.

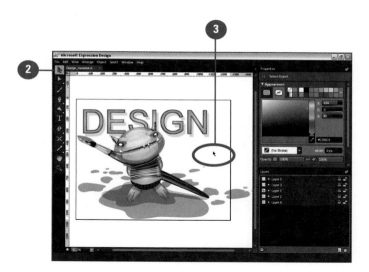

Working with Objects

Introduction

Every piece of artwork you create in Expression Design is made up of objects. This includes all shapes, paths, text, and imported graphics that you include in your designs.

In this chapter you'll learn the various ways to move objects around in your documents. This includes clicking and dragging objects with the different selection-making tools, entering precise horizontal and vertical pivot point coordinates in the Action bar, and nudging objects incrementally with the arrow keys.

You'll also learn how to reposition objects using Expression Design's powerful Distribute, Stack, and Align commands. These features allow you to line up objects evenly and apply an even amount of space between their edges or center points. In addition, you'll learn the benefit of locking objects as you edit neighboring graphic items, as well as how to unlock them all at once.

This chapter also demonstrates the different ways you can duplicate selected objects. This includes duplicating by Alt+dragging, copying and pasting objects, and applying the Duplicate command. Finally, you'll discover how to group, ungroup, and delete objects in Expression Design.

What You'll Do

Move Objects with Selection Tools

Move Objects with the Action Bar

Nudge Objects

Arrange Objects with Order Commands

Distribute Objects

Stack Objects

Align Objects

Lock Objects

Unlock All

Duplicate Objects with the Duplicate Command

Duplicate by Alt+Dragging

Copy and Paste Objects

Group and Ungroup

Delete Objects

Moving Objects with the Selection Tools

The various selection tools (Selection, Direct Selection, Lasso Selection, and Group Select) can be used not only to select objects, but also to reposition them in the document. This is the quickest and easiest way to move objects as you create graphics in Expression Design.

Click and Drag Objects Using the Various Selection Tools

1 Access any of the selection tools (Selection, Direct Selection, Lasso Selection, or Group Select) by clicking its icon in the **Tools** panel.

2 Select an object (or objects) using any of the selection methods described in Chapter 5, "Making Selections."

3 Click and drag the selected object(s) to a different area of the document. To constrain your movements to 45° angles, hold down the **Shift** key as you drag.

Did You Know?

The Quick (area) Select option controls how the selection tools behave. With the Quick (area) Select option enabled (located in the General pane of the Options dialog box), clicking and dragging with any of the selection tools allows you to select and move an object all in one fast motion. When disabled, clicking and dragging creates a marquee selection.

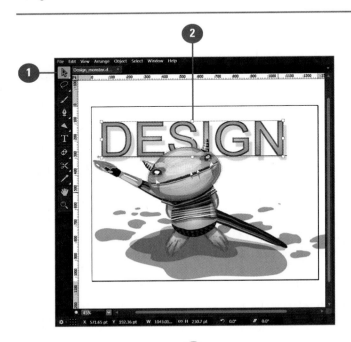

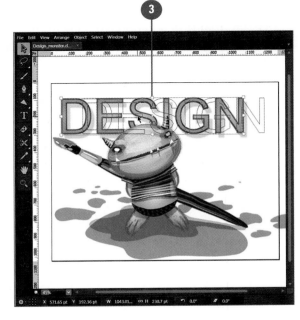

Moving Objects with the Action Bar

A more precise alternative to moving objects with the various selection tools is to reposition them using the Action bar. By entering specific horizontal and vertical coordinates in the X and Y fields of the Action bar, you can control where the registration (or pivot) point of the object is positioned.

Enter New X and Y Coordinates

1. Select an object (or objects) using any of the selection methods described in Chapter 5, "Making Selections."

2. The Action bar displays the exact X and Y coordinates for the currently selected object(s). The X and Y values determine the exact position of the currently selected object's registration (or pivot) point (center by default).

   IMPORTANT *You can change the registration point by clicking any of the white squares in the Registration Point icon located on the far left of the Action bar.*

3. To reposition the selected object(s) precisely in the document, enter new coordinates into the X and Y fields of the Action bar.

See Also

See Chapter 5, "Making Selections," to learn more about selecting objects in Expression Design.

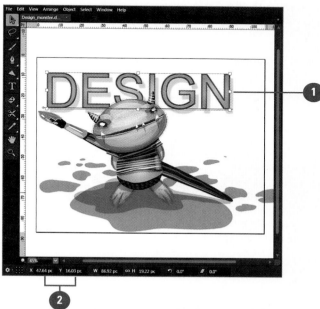

Nudging Objects

Another quick and easy way to move selected objects is to nudge them with the arrow keys. Generally, nudging is a technique used to move an object a very short distance. Because of this, the default nudge increment value is very low; however, you can increase it by changing the setting in the Options dialog box.

Nudge with the Arrow Keys

1 Select an object (or objects) using any of the selection methods described in Chapter 5, "Making Selections."

2 Press the arrow keys to nudge the selected object(s) in a specific direction (up, down, left, or right).

3 The amount of space applied when nudging a selected object (or objects) is determined by the value entered in the **Nudge Increment** field. You can access this setting in the **Units and Grids** pane of the **Options** dialog box.

Did You Know?

The Nudge Increment option uses the same measurement unit as the Document Units option. In the Units and Grids pane of the Options dialog box, the measurement unit that you choose in the Document Units field determines what measurement unit is displayed in the neighboring Nudge Increment field.

Holding down Shift as you nudge with the arrow keys increases the distance by ten times. You can quickly move selected objects much farther by holding down Shift as you nudge with the arrow keys.

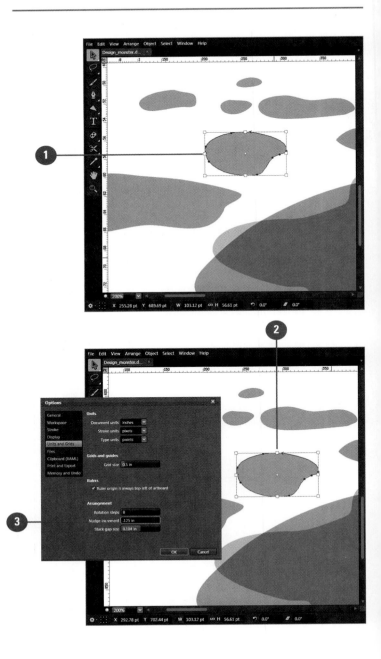

Arranging Objects with Order Commands

The Order commands (Bring to Front, Bring Forward, Send Backward, and Send to Back) allow you to rearrange the stacking order of objects contained within a single layer. These commands are especially useful when working with overlapping objects that collectively make up a single graphic or design.

Bring to Front

1. Use the shape tools (Rectangle, Ellipse, and Polygon) to create three distinctly different shapes.

2. Select and reposition each shape to create a stack of overlapping objects.

3. Select the bottom object. Then under the **Arrange** menu, choose **Order** and select **Bring to Front** from the fly-out menu.

   TIMESAVER *Press Ctrl+Shift+] to apply the Bring to Front command quickly.*

   The selected object now appears at the top of the stack rather than at the bottom.

> ### Did You Know?
>
> *You can also access the Order commands from the contextual menu.* To access the Order commands from the contextual menu, make sure you have multiple objects selected and then right-click and choose the command from the Arrange submenu.

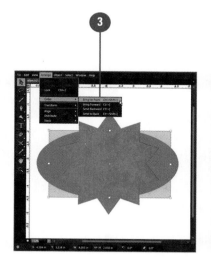

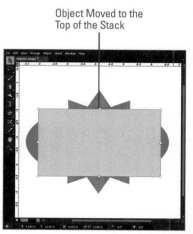

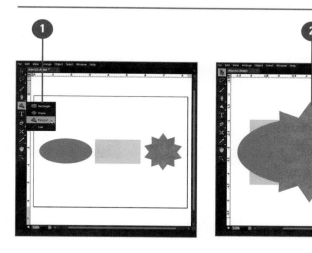

Object Moved to the Top of the Stack

Bring Forward

1 Select the bottom or middle object. Then under the **Arrange** menu, choose **Order** and select **Bring Forward** from the fly-out menu.

TIMESAVER *Press Ctrl+] to apply the Bring Forward command quickly.*

The selected object now appears on top of the object that was previously above it in the stack.

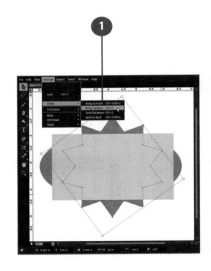

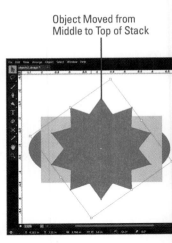

Object Moved from Middle to Top of Stack

Send Backward

1 Select the top or middle object. Then under the **Arrange** menu, choose **Order** and select **Send Backward** from the fly-out menu.

TIMESAVER *Press Ctrl+[to apply the Send Backward command quickly.*

The selected object now appears beneath the object that was previously below it in the stack.

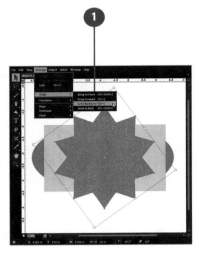

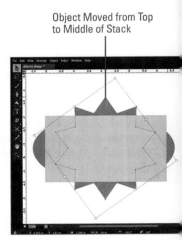

Object Moved from Top to Middle of Stack

Send to Back

1 Select the top object. Then under the **Arrange** menu, choose **Order** and select **Send to Back** from the fly-out menu.

TIMESAVER *Press Ctrl+Shift+]*
to apply the Send to Back
command quickly.

The selected object now appears at the bottom of the stack rather than at the top.

Did You Know?

Applying the Order commands con-
trols the stacking order of objects in
the Layers panel. Applying the Order commands has the same effect as changing the stacking order of objects in the Layers panel.

See Also

See Chapter 7,"Working with Layers,"
to learn more about arranging objects
with layers in Expression Design.

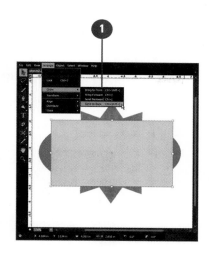

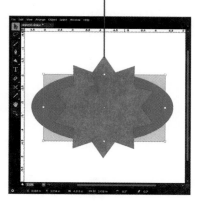

Object Moved to
Bottom of Stack

Distributing Objects

The Distribute commands allow you to control precisely where selected objects are placed in relation to each other in a document. With these commands, Expression Design calculates the amount of space currently between each selected object's edge or center point and then repositions them so that they are spaced evenly.

Apply the Distribute Commands

1 Select three or more objects using any of the selection methods described in Chapter 5, "Making Selections."

2 Choose **Distribute** from the **Arrange** menu, and select any of the available commands from the fly-out submenu.

> **TIMESAVER** *You can also access the Distribute commands from the pop-up list available in the Action bar.*

The objects are distributed evenly from edge to edge or from center point to center point (depending on which command you choose).

> **IMPORTANT** *Unless the selected objects are exactly the same size, the amount of space placed between the edges of each object might not appear the same when applying the Distribute commands. To apply the same amount of spacing between object edges, you must apply one of the Stacking commands.*

Did You Know?

The farthest object always stays in place. When applying any of the Distribute, Stack, or Align commands, the farthest selected object remains in position. For example, when choosing Top Edges, the top object remains in place while the others are repositioned.

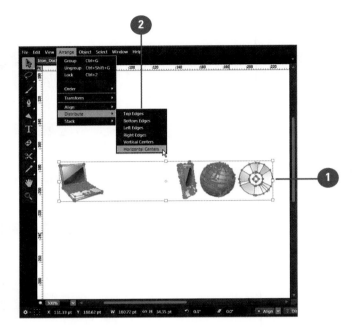

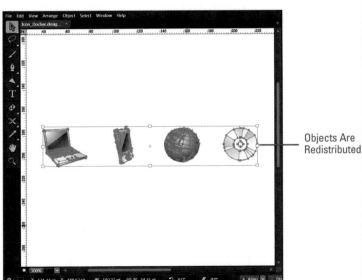

Objects Are Redistributed

Stacking Objects

The Stack commands are similar to the Distribute commands in that they also allow you to control precisely where objects are placed in relation to each other in the document. The difference is that the Stack commands allow you to specify and apply an exact amount of space between each selected object.

Apply the Stack Commands

1. Select three or more objects using any of the selection methods described in Chapter 5, "Making Selections."

2. Choose **Stack** from the **Arrange** menu, and select any of the available commands from the fly-out submenu.

   TIMESAVER *You can also access the Stack commands from the pop-up list available in the Action bar.*

3. The space between object edges is distributed evenly using the value entered in the **Stack Gap Size** field. You can access this setting in the **Units and Grids** pane of the **Options** dialog box.

Did You Know?

The Stack Gap Size option uses the same measurement unit as the Document Units option. In the Units and Grids pane of the Options dialog box, the measurement unit that you choose in the Document Units field determines what measurement unit is displayed in the Stack Gap Size field.

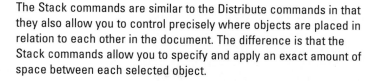
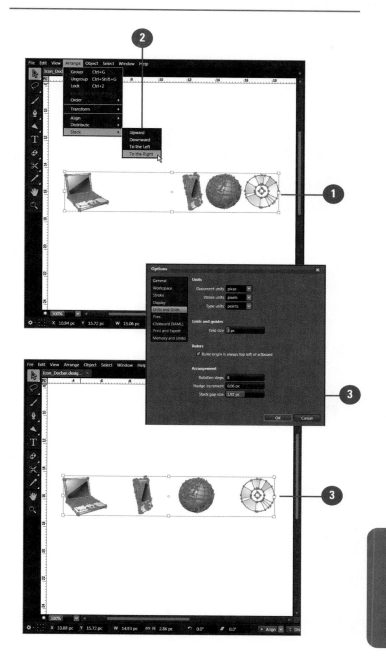

Aligning Objects

In Chapter 4, "Working with Grids, Guides, and Points" you learned how to align objects using ruler guides, the document grid, and the Snap to Point feature. In addition to applying those useful techniques, you can also align selected objects by applying the Align commands. Doing so aligns the objects evenly in relation to each other in the document.

Apply the Align Commands

1 Select two or more objects using any of the selection methods described in Chapter 5, "Making Selections."

2 Choose **Align** from the **Arrange** menu, and select any of the available commands from the fly-out submenu.

TIMESAVER *You can also access the Align commands from the pop up-list available in the Action bar.*

The objects are aligned evenly from edge to edge or from center point to center point (depending on which command you choose).

Did You Know?

Applying the Align Centers command creates a stack of objects. When you apply the Align Centers command, all the selected objects are stacked on top of each other, and their center points are perfectly aligned.

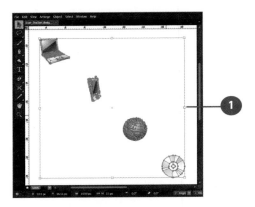

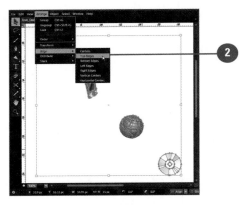

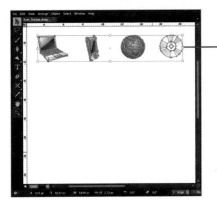

Objects Are Realigned

Locking Objects

By applying the Lock command to a specific selected object, you can ensure that it will not be accidentally moved or transformed as you work with neighboring graphic elements. As your graphics develop and become more complicated, you will gradually start to rely on the Lock command for preventive maintenance.

Apply the Lock Command

① Select an object (or objects) using any of the selection methods described in Chapter 5, "Making Selections."

② Under the **Arrange** menu, choose **Lock.**

> **TIMESAVER** *Press Ctrl+2 to apply the Lock command quickly.*

Expression Design locks the object(s) into position so that it can no longer be selected in the document. The respective lock icons for each object also appear closed in the Layers panel.

See Also

See Chapter 7,"Working with Layers," to learn more about locking objects with layers in Expression Design.

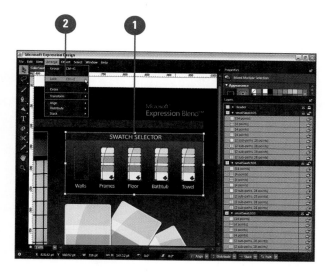

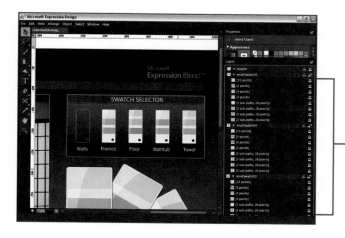

Objects with Closed Padlock Are Locked

Unlocking All

Locking objects is a great way to ensure their positions on the artboard, but doing so does not allow you to move or transform them. At some point you might need to unlock all the locked items in your artwork to edit them. In Expression Design, you can unlock all the locked objects in the document at once by applying the Unlock All command.

Apply the Unlock All Command

1 Under the **Arrange** menu, choose **Unlock All**.

> **TIMESAVER** *Press Ctrl+Alt+2 to apply the Unlock All command quickly.*

All the locked objects in the document become unlocked and can now be selected. All the lock icons in the Layers panel also appear open.

Did You Know?

You can unlock individual locked objects using the lock toggles in the Layers panel. If you'd like to unlock a specific object without unlocking everything, you can do so by clicking the object's lock icon in the Layers panel or by right-clicking the object and choosing Unlock from the contextual menu.

See Also

See Chapter 7,"Working with Layers," to learn more about unlocking objects with layers in Expression Design.

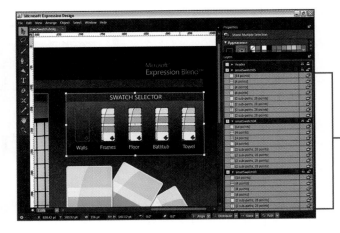

Objects Are All Unlocked

Duplicating Objects with the Duplicate Command

It's not uncommon for a series of graphic icons or interface items to contain similar shapes and paths. As you create these types of graphics in Expression Design, you can work more efficiently by duplicating common or shared elements. By applying the Duplicate command, you can copy and reuse selected objects in your documents.

Apply the Duplicate Command

① Select an object (or objects) using any of the selection methods described in Chapter 5, "Making Selections."

② Under the **Edit** menu, choose **Duplicate**.

Expression Design duplicates the selected object and places it above and to the right of the original object, and at the top of the stacking order in the Layers panel.

See Also

See Chapter 7, "Working with Layers," to learn more about duplicating objects with layers in Expression Design.

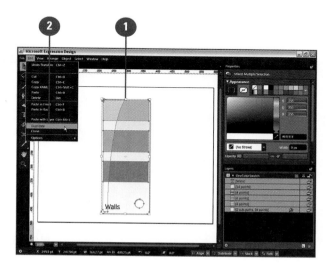

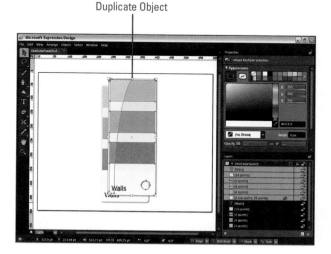

Duplicate Object

Duplicating by Alt+Dragging

One quick way to duplicate objects on the fly is to select and Alt+drag them. The Alt key serves as a temporary modifier when working with any of the various selection tools in Expression Design. By holding down Alt as you click and drag an object, you make a copy of it.

Alt+Drag to Duplicate a Selected Object

1. Select an object (or objects) using any of the selection methods described in Chapter 5, "Making Selections."

2. Hold down the **Alt** key. As you do, the tool's cursor changes to display two arrows: one black and one white. This is Expression Design's way of telling you that you've temporarily modified the tool with a keyboard shortcut.

3. With the **Alt** key held down, click and drag in any direction to duplicate the selected object(s).

Did You Know?

Alt+dragging does not position the duplicate object at the top of the stack. Unlike the Duplicate command, which places the duplicate object at the top of the stack, Alt+dragging places the duplicate object directly above the original object in the stacking order.

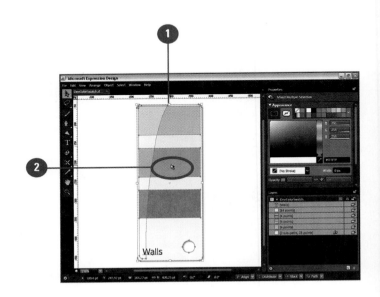

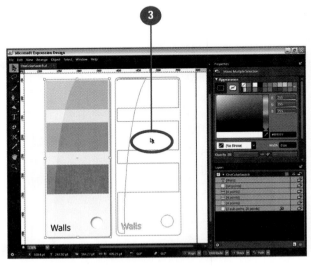

Copying and Pasting Objects

You can also duplicate objects by applying the Copy and Paste commands. Doing so copies the object to your computer's clipboard, which makes this technique especially useful when copying and pasting objects into other Expression Design documents. The Paste in Front and Paste in Back commands allow you to place the duplicate object in the same position on the artboard as the original and also control its stacking order.

Apply the Copy/Paste Commands

① Select an object (or objects) using any of the selection methods described in Chapter 5, "Making Selections."

② Under the **Edit** menu, choose **Copy**. Expression Design copies the object to the Clipboard.

> **TIMESAVER** *Press Ctrl+C to apply the Copy command quickly.*

> **IMPORTANT** *To copy an object and also remove it from the document, press Ctrl+X to apply the Cut command.*

③ Under the **Edit** menu, choose **Paste**.

> **TIMESAVER** *Press Ctrl+V to apply the Paste command quickly.*

Expression Design places the pasted object in the center of the document and at the top of the stacking order in the Layers panel.

Did You Know?

You can control the stacking order of pasted objects. To ensure that the pasted object is positioned directly above or below the copied object in the stacking order, make sure to keep the original copied object selected and choose Paste in Front or Paste in Back from the Edit menu.

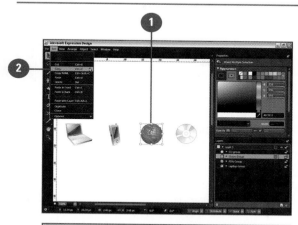

Pasted Object

Grouping and Ungrouping

Grouping multiple selected objects together allows you to move and transform them collectively, rather than one by one. This is a great technique for repositioning objects such as web buttons, text items, or interface controls that have already been aligned. Individual objects can be selected from within the group using the Group Select, Direct Selection, or Lasso Selection tools.

Apply the Group and Ungroup Commands

1 Select two or more objects using any of the selection methods described in Chapter 5, "Making Selections."

2 Choose **Group** from the **Arrange** menu, or right-click the selection and choose **Group** from the contextual menu.

TIMESAVER *Press Ctrl+G to apply the Group command quickly.*

3 The objects are grouped together and can now be moved and transformed collectively. They are also labeled as a group in the Layers panel.

4 To ungroup the objects, choose **Ungroup** from the **Arrange** menu or the contextual menu.

TIMESAVER *Press Ctrl+Shift+G to apply the Ungroup command quickly.*

Did You Know?

You cannot create a group containing objects that are placed on separate layers. To create a group, all the selected objects must reside on the same layer.

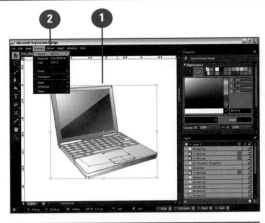

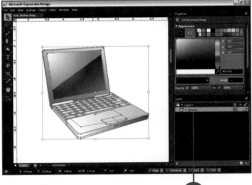

Deleting Objects

The Delete command allows you to completely remove selected objects from the document. As with most other applications, you can press the Delete or Backspace keys to apply the Delete command.

Apply the Delete Command

1. Select an object (or objects) using any of the selection methods described in Chapter 5, "Making Selections."

2. Under the **Edit** menu, choose **Delete.**

   TIMESAVER *Press Delete or Backspace to apply the Delete command quickly.*

   The object(s) are removed from the document immediately.

See Also

See Chapter 7,"Working with Layers," to learn about deleting objects with layers in Expression Design.

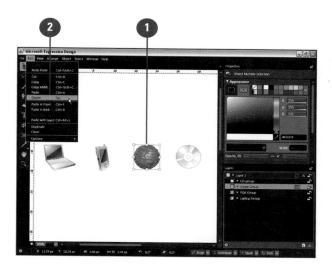

Object Is Removed

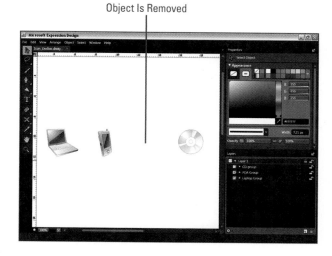

Working with Layers

Introduction

The Layers panel is an incredibly powerful tool in Expression Design. Not only can you use layers to rearrange the stacking order of objects in a document, but you can also use the various controls in the Layers panel to select, duplicate, and delete objects. The Layers panel also includes toggle controls for locking and unlocking objects and toggling their visibility.

You can categorize specific objects in a document by placing them on different layers. Doing so allows you to sample different design ideas by toggling visibility for objects that are placed on different layers.

In this chapter, you'll learn how to use all the controls available in the Layers panel. You'll learn how to create and name new layers, as well as how to label individual objects within a layer. In addition, you'll learn how to select individual objects and groups of objects directly from the Layers panel and how to use the lock and visibility toggles.

This chapter also walks you through the various Layers panel options, including changing layer color, choosing a different layer render style, adjusting layer thumbnail options, and previewing objects as bitmap graphics by freezing a layer.

What You'll Do

Create New Layers

Name Layers and Layer Objects

Show/Hide Layer Objects in the Layers Panel

Toggle Layer Visibility

Select with Layers

Arrange Objects with Layers

Copy and Paste into a Different Layer

Copy and Paste with Layers

Lock Objects with Layers

Duplicate with Layers

Delete with Layers

Change Layer Color Options

Change Layer Render Style

Freeze a Layer

Change Layer Thumbnail Options

Creating New Layers

To place objects on separate layers, you must first create the layers in the document. In Expression Design you can add layers two different ways: by clicking the New Layer icon or by choosing the New Layer option from the Layer Options pop-up menu. Both are accessible from the bottom of the Layers panel.

Click the New Layer Icon

① If it is not already visible onscreen, display the Layers panel by choosing **Layers** from the **Window** menu. If a check mark is currently displayed next to the word **Layers,** it is already open.

TIMESAVER *Press F4 to quickly hide or show the Layers panel.*

② Click the **New Layer** icon located in the bottom-right corner of the Layers panel.

The new layer appears above the currently selected layer in the Layers panel.

> ### Did You Know?
>
> ***All Expression Design documents contain at least one layer.*** Every new document that you create in Expression Design contains a single layer, which is named "Layer 1" by default. You can add and delete as many layers as you like, but you must always keep at least one in the Layers panel.

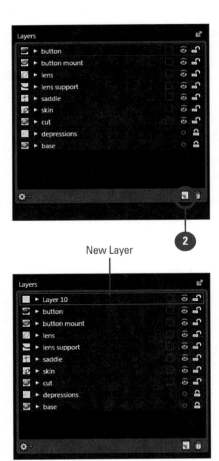

New Layer

Choose the New Layer Option

1 Click the **Layer Option** icon located in the bottom-left corner of the Layers panel.

2 Choose **New Layer** from the fly-out menu that appears.

The new layer appears above the currently selected layer in the Layers panel.

Did You Know?

You can choose to always add new layers at the top of the Layers panel list. If you'd like to always add new layers at the top of the Layers panel list (rather than above the currently selected layer), disable the Create New Layer Above Current Layer option in the General panel of the Options dialog box.

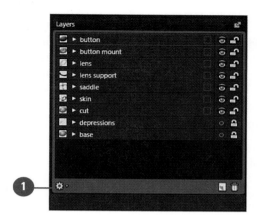

New Layer

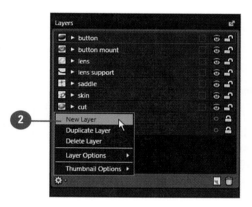

Naming Layers and Layer Objects

A good habit to get into when working with multiple layers is to name them accordingly. Doing so can make it much easier to locate the objects you'd like to work with in your documents, especially if they contain extensive amounts of detailed graphics and text. You might also find it helpful to label certain layer objects contained within each layer.

Rename a Layer

1. Double-click the layer name in the **Layers** panel to highlight it. By default, all new layers are automatically named "Layer 1," "Layer 2," and so forth.

2. Enter a new name for the layer and press **Enter.**

> ### Did You Know?
>
> ***Always name your layers something logical.*** By giving your layers logical names, such as "Text Links" or "Interface Controls," it will be much easier for you to locate them in the Layers panel as you work.

Rename a Layer Object

1. In the **Layers** panel, click the toggle arrow to the left of the layer name. Doing so displays a vertical list in the Layers panel of objects contained within that layer. This indicates the stacking order of the layer objects.

2. Double-click the layer object name in the **Layers** panel to highlight it. By default, all layer objects are automatically named based on the number of points that make up the object's path.

3. Enter a new name for the layer object and press **Enter.**

> ### See Also
>
> *See Chapter 8,"Drawing Shapes and Paths," to learn more about using the drawing tools in Expression Design.*

Showing/Hiding Layer Objects in the Layers Panel

You can display a vertical list in the Layers panel of all of the objects placed on each layer by clicking the toggle arrow next to each layer name. This reveals the stacking order of objects in the document and can make it much easier for you to arrange them using the Order commands or by repositioning the layers or layer objects in the Layers panel. If showing layer objects starts to take up too much room in the Layers panel, simply resize the panel or hide layer objects by clicking the toggle arrows.

Show or Hide Layer Objects with the Toggle Arrow

① In the **Layers** panel, click the toggle arrow to the left of the layer name.

IMPORTANT *You can click the toggle arrows without having to select the layer or the layer object first.*

② All the objects contained within the layer are revealed in the Layers panel. Expression Design displays the objects in their current stacking order.

③ Click the layer toggle arrow again to hide the objects in the Layers panel.

Did You Know?

You can only select one layer at a time. Expression Design only allows you to select one layer at a time in the Layers panel. You can identify which layer is currently selected by the color outline that is displayed around it.

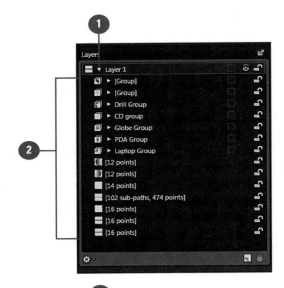

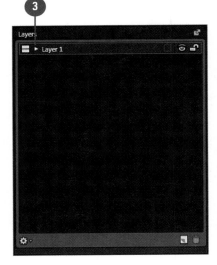

Toggling Layer Visibility

You can hide and show objects placed on specific layers by clicking the visibility toggles located in the Layers panel. Doing so can help you focus on specific objects within your artwork. After the objects are hidden, they cannot be selected in the document. Note also that you cannot toggle visibility for individual layer objects within a layer.

Hide and Show Objects Using the Layer Visibility Toggles

1. In the **Layers** panel, point to the visibility toggle (the eye icon) for the layer containing the objects you'd like to hide.

   IMPORTANT *It is not necessary to select the layer in the Layers panel to toggle its visibility.*

2. Click the eye icon to hide all the objects placed on that layer. When the objects are hidden, the eye icon disappears from the Layers panel and is replaced by a small gray circle. Click the small gray circle to make the hidden objects visible again.

   TIMESAVER *To hide all layers except the one you'd like to view, Alt+click the eye icon for that layer. Alt+click the eye icon again to show all hidden layers.*

Did You Know?

Hidden objects cannot be selected. Expression Design automatically locks all hidden layers.

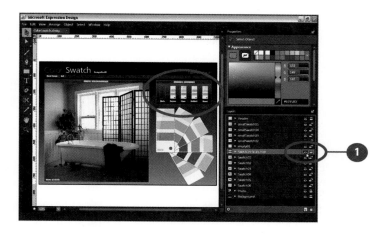

Selecting with Layers

The Layers panel can also be a useful tool for making selections. By clicking one of the selection square icons to the right of a layer's name, you can select all the objects contained within that layer. To select individual objects on a specific layer, you must reveal them in the Layers panel and then click the layer object. This is especially useful when attempting to select objects that are stacked directly on top of each other in the document, as these types of arrangements can make locating the correct object with one of the selection-making tools very difficult.

Select All Layer Objects

1. In the **Layers** panel, click the small square to the right of the layer name. Doing so selects all the objects contained within that layer in the document. Expression Design displays a color fill in the selection square for that layer.

   IMPORTANT *It is not necessary to select the layer in the Layers panel to select its contents.*

   Expression Design outlines the edges of the selected objects with the assigned layer color in the document. If you have the Selection tool accessed, Expression Design also displays a bounding box around the selected objects in the document.

Selected Object Outlined in Layer Color

Did You Know?

Every layer is assigned its own color. Expression Design automatically assigns a different color to each layer that you add. This is the color that is displayed in the selection square for the layer in the Layers panel and around the object when showing Edges (under the View menu, choose Edges from the Show fly-out submenu).

Select Individual Layer Objects

1 In the **Layers** panel, click the toggle arrow to the left of the layer name. Doing so displays a vertical list of objects contained within that layer in the Layers panel. This indicates the stacking order of the layer objects.

2 Click the layer object name in the **Layers** panel to select it in the document.

3 Shift+click multiple layer object names in the **Layers** panel (including those in other layers) to select multiple objects in the document.

Expression Design displays a color fill inside (or outline around) the selection square for the layer in the Layers panel and outlines the edge of the selected objects with the same color in the document. If you have the Selection tool accessed, Expression Design also displays a bounding box around the selected objects in the document.

Did You Know?

Layer selection squares: solid color versus colored outline. Expression Design displays a solid color in the layer selection square when all objects in the layer (or a grouped or masked layer object) are selected. It displays a colored outline around the layer selection square when some (but not all) of the objects in the layer are selected.

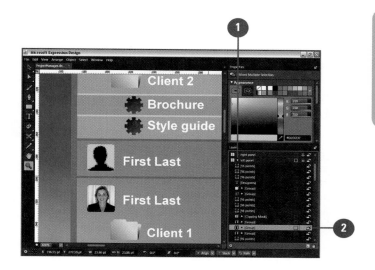

Selected Objects

Arranging Objects with Layers

Layers are also excellent arranging tools. By placing objects on separate layers, you can control their stacking order in the document. You can also control the stacking order of objects within a layer by repositioning the layer objects in the Layers panel.

Reposition Layer Objects in the Layers Panel

1. In the **Layers** panel, click the toggle arrow to the left of the layer name. Doing so displays a vertical list of objects contained within that layer in the Layers panel. This indicates the stacking order of the layer objects.

2. Click any layer object name in the **Layers** panel to select it in the document. You can also Shift+click to select multiple layer objects.

3. In the **Layers** panel, drag the selected layer object(s) to a different position within the layer or to a different layer altogether.

   The object is now displayed in the document in its new stacking order.

> ### Did You Know?
>
> **You can change the stacking order of multiple objects in a document by repositioning a layer in the Layers panel.** When you select and move a layer (which includes all its layer objects), you can reposition the stacking order of the layer objects that it contains in the document.

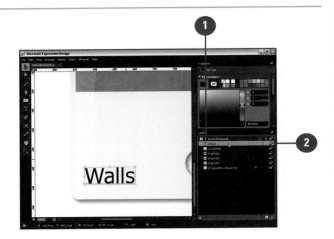

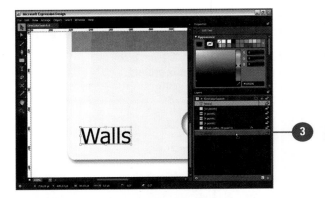

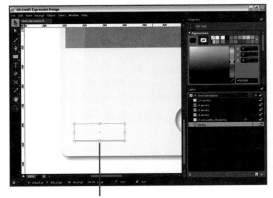

New Stacking Order

Copying and Pasting into a Different Layer

One way you can duplicate objects and control their stacking order at the same time is to copy and paste them into different layers. All you need to do is copy the selected object using the Copy command and then select a different layer (or create one if necessary) and apply the Paste command.

Apply the Copy and Paste Commands with Layers

① Click any layer or layer object name in the **Layers** panel to select the object(s) in the document.

② Choose **Copy** from the **Edit** menu to copy the object(s) to the Clipboard.

TIMESAVER *Press Ctrl+C to apply the Copy command quickly.*

③ Select a different layer in the **Layers** panel.

④ Choose **Paste** from the **Edit** menu.

TIMESAVER *Press Ctrl+V to apply the Paste command quickly.*

Expression Design places the pasted object in the center of the document and at the top of the stacking order in the layer.

See Also

See Chapter 6, "Working with Objects," to learn more about copying and pasting objects in Expression Design.

Pasted Object

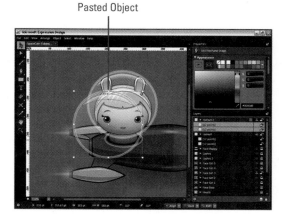

Copying and Pasting with Layers

By applying the Paste with Layers command, you can maintain your layer structure when copying multiple objects from one Expression Design document to another. This is a great way to stay organized when copying and pasting detailed graphics into multiple documents.

Apply the Copy and Paste with Layer Commands

① Select multiple objects that are placed on different layers in a document.

② Choose **Copy** from the **Edit** menu to copy the objects to the Clipboard.

TIMESAVER *Press Ctrl+C to apply the Copy command quickly.*

③ Press Ctrl+N to create a new document. In the New Document dialog box that appears, choose a preset document size from the **Presets** list or enter specific width and height values in the fields provided.

④ Click **OK** to create the new document.

⑤ Press **Ctrl+Atl+L** or choose **Paste with Layer** from the **Edit** menu. Expression Design places the pasted object in its own layer in the center of the document. The layer also retains its name from the original document.

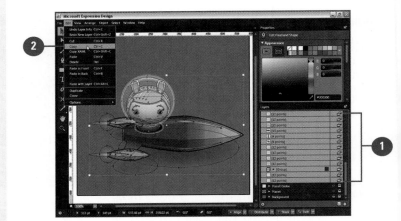

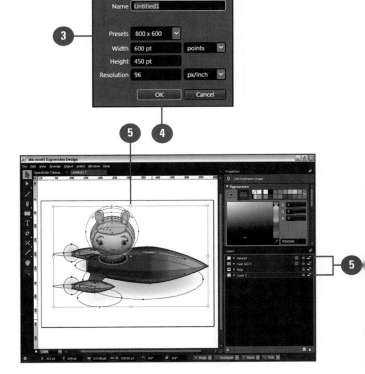

Locking Objects with Layers

In Expression Design, every layer and layer object in the Layers panel contains its own lock toggle. Locking and unlocking objects this way offers you much more control than applying the Lock and Unlock All commands. Not only can you unlock individual layer objects using this method (as opposed to unlocking all), but you can also lock and unlock groups of objects contained within a layer all at once, without having to select them first.

Locking Individual Layer Objects

1. In the **Layers** panel, point to the open lock toggle icon for the layer object that you'd like to lock.

    IMPORTANT *You do not have to select the layer in the Layers panel first to lock it with the toggle.*

2. Click the lock toggle to lock the layer object in the document. The lock icon appears closed in the Layers panel. The object is now locked into position and can no longer be selected in the document.

    Click the lock toggle again to unlock the object. The lock icon now appears open in the Layers panel, and the object can be selected.

Did You Know?

Selection squares are not displayed in the Layers panel for locked layers. Because they cannot be selected, Expression Design does not display a selection square in the Layers panel for locked layers.

Lock All Layer Objects

In the **Layers** panel, point to the lock toggle icon for the layer containing the objects that you'd like to lock.

Click the lock toggle icon to lock all of the objects placed on that layer. The lock icon appears closed in the Layers panel, and (when shown) the lock icons for its layer objects also appear grayed out. The objects are now locked into position and can no longer be selected in the document.

Click the lock toggle icon again to unlock all the objects. The lock icon now appears open in the Layers panel, and the objects can be selected.

See Also

See Chapter 6, "Working with Objects," to learn more about locking objects in Expression Design.

Duplicating with Layers

Another way you can duplicate selected objects and place them into different layers (besides applying the Copy/Paste commands) is to Alt+drag the layer selection square into a different layer in the Layers panel. This is generally a much quicker way to duplicate objects and control their stacking order at the same time.

Duplicate Using the Selection Square

1 Select an object that you'd like to duplicate in the document. If there is more than one object on that layer, Expression Design displays a colored outline around the layer selection square to the right of the layer name. If it is the only object on the layer, Expression Design displays a solid color fill in the selection square.

2 Alt+drag the selection square to a different layer in the Layers panel. Expression Design displays a + symbol next to the cursor as you Alt+drag. Release the mouse button to add the duplicate object to the layer.

The duplicate object remains selected in the document, and the layer that you Alt+dragged to becomes selected in the Layers panel.

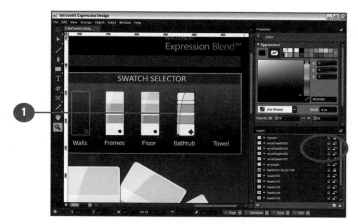

Did You Know?

You can Alt+drag multiple selected objects in the Layers panel. To duplicate multiple selected objects, Shift+click the various layer objects in the Layers panel (from a single layer only—not multiple layers) and Alt+drag the selection square to a different layer.

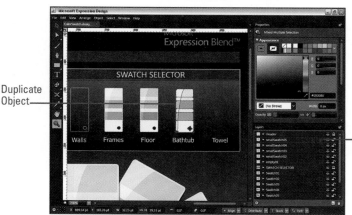

Duplicate Object

Selected Layer

Deleting with Layers

In addition to the Delete command, Expression Design also allows you to delete objects using the delete controls in the Layers panel. By selecting a layer and clicking the Delete Layer icon or choosing the Delete Layer option, you can remove all the objects contained in that layer from the document at once.

Remove Layers with the Delete Layer Icon

1 In the **Layers** panel, select the layer containing the objects that you'd like to delete. Note that you only have to select the layer. It is not necessary to select all the layer's contents by clicking the selection square first.

IMPORTANT *Expression Design only allows you to select one layer at a time in the Layers panel.*

2 Click the **Delete Layer** icon located in the bottom-right corner of the **Layers** panel.

3 When the Delete Layer warning dialog box appears, click **Yes.**

The objects are deleted from the document, and the layer is removed from the Layers panel.

Did You Know?

You cannot delete layer objects using the controls in the Layers panel. If you select a layer object and click the Delete layer icon or choose Delete Layer from the Layer Option fly-out menu, Expression Design deletes the entire layer (except Layer 1) and all its contents—not just the selected object.

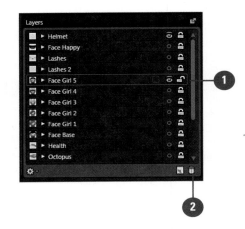

Objects Are Deleted

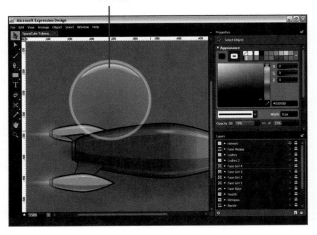

Choose the Delete Layer Option

① In the **Layers** panel, select the layer containing the objects that you'd like to delete.

② Click the **Layer Option** icon located in the bottom-left corner of the **Layers** panel.

③ Choose **Delete Layer** from the fly-out menu that appears.

④ When the Delete Layer warning dialog box appears, click **Yes**.

The objects are deleted from the document, and the layer is removed from the Layers panel.

Did You Know?

You can delete locked layers using the delete controls in the Layers panel. Expression Design does allow you to select a locked layer and delete it by clicking the Delete Layer icon or by choosing Delete Layer from the Layer Option fly-out menu.

See Also

See Chapter 6,"Working with Objects," to learn more about deleting objects in Expression Design.

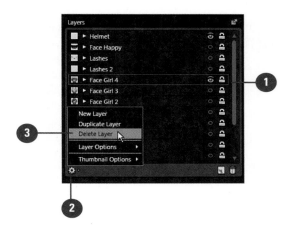

Objects Are Deleted

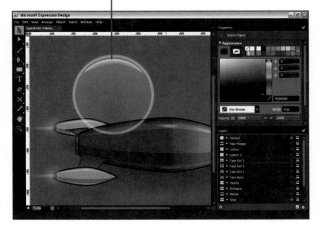

Changing Layer Color Options

Expression Design automatically assigns a different color to each layer that you create. This is the color that is displayed around the layer when it is selected in the Layers panel and is also the color that is displayed around any objects that reside on that layer when you select them in the document. If the layer color is too similar to the applied stroke or fill color of the selected object, you might want to assign a different color to the layer.

Change the Layer Color Option

1. In the **Layers** panel, select a layer that contains a highlight color that conflicts with the objects in the document.

2. Click the **Layer Option** icon located in the bottom-left corner of the **Layers** panel.

3. Choose **Layer Options** from the fly-out menu that appears and select **Layer Color** from the fly-out submenu.

4. In the Color Picker window that appears, choose a different color for the layer using any of the following methods:

   ◆ **RGB fields**—Enter specific values in the corresponding R, G, B fields.

   ◆ **Hex Value field**—Enter the hexidecimal code for the chosen color in the Hex Value field.

   ◆ **Color Dropper tool**—Sample a color with the Color Dropper tool.

   ◆ **Hue bar slider**—Move the vertical hue bar slider to choose a color range and select the hue by moving the circle icon.

5. Click anywhere in the document to hide the Color Picker window and apply the highlight color to the layer.

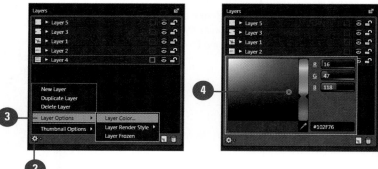

Changing Layer Render Style

As described in Chapter 1, "Getting Started with Expression Design," you can set the default document Display Quality setting by choosing one of the options under the View menu: Preview (all attributes displayed) or Wireframe (all attributes hidden except bitmap brushstrokes). By default, the Layer Render Style for all layers is the same as the Display Quality settting; however, you can choose to change the Layer Render Style for a selected layer at any time. This feature allows you to view specific objects in one mode, such as Wireframe or Path (with all attributes hidden, including bitmap brushstrokes), while the rest of the objects in the document are displayed in an entirely different mode, such as Preview.

Change the Layer Render Style Option

1. In the **Layers** panel, select the layer containing the objects that you'd like to view in the document using a different render style.

   IMPORTANT *When changing layer render style, you only have to select the layer. It is not necessary to select all the layer's contents by clicking the selection square first.*

2. Click the **Layer Option** icon located in the bottom-left corner of the **Layers** panel.

3. Choose **Layer Options** from the fly-out menu that appears.

4. Select **Layer Render Style** from the fly-out submenu. Choose a different render style from the submenu. Options include Default, Path, Wireframe, and Preview.

   All objects contained within the layer are displayed in the document window using the new render style option.

   IMPORTANT *The default render style is determined by the option that is chosen from the Display Quality submenu, which is located under the View menu. Options include Wireframe and Preview.*

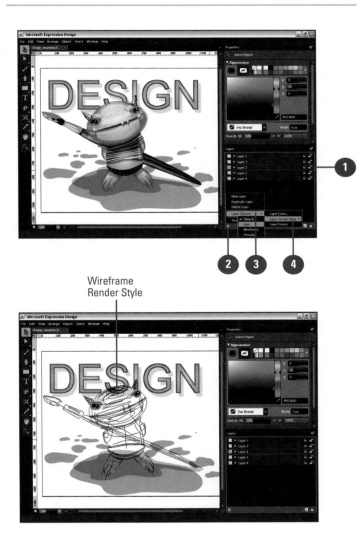

Wireframe
Render Style

Freezing a Layer

Expression Design is unique in that it allows you to create both vector and bitmap graphics. By nature it is a vector-drawing application, but it also allows you to save the artwork you create as a bitmap graphic. You can preview what the objects on a specific layer will look like when saved as a bitmap by freezing the layer.

Apply the Layer Frozen Option

① In the Layers panel, select the layer that you'd like to freeze.

② Click the **Layer Option** icon located in the bottom-left corner of the **Layers** panel.

③ Choose **Layer Options** from the fly-out menu that appears and select **Layer Frozen** from the fly-out submenu.

④ If any of the objects contained within the layer have blend modes applied, a warning dialog appears to let you know that the preview might be inaccurate. Click **Yes** to bypass the warning dialog and freeze the layer.

In the document window, Expression Design displays a bitmap preview of the objects contained within the frozen layer. In addition, the layer is automatically locked in the Layers panel and appears with a striped pattern to indicate that it is frozen.

IMPORTANT *The frozen bitmap preview uses the resolution setting that is currently applied to the document. You can change the document resolution setting in the Document Size dialog box, which is accessible under the File menu.*

⑤ To unfreeze the layer, choose **Layer Frozen** from the **Layer Options** submenu or click the layer's lock toggle icon.

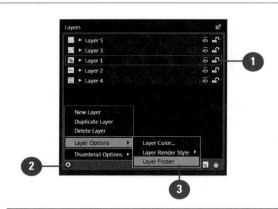

Bitmap Preview

Changing Layer Thumbnail Options

By default, Expression Design displays a thumbnail to the left of each layer's name in the Layers panel. Each thumbnail displays a small visual representation of the layer's contents. You can determine the size of the layer thumbnails by choosing an option from the Layer Options pop-up menu, or you can choose not to display them at all. There is also a Popup Thumbnails option that, similar to tooltips, causes a thumbnail to appear when you hover the cursor over a layer or layer object.

Change the Layers Panel Thumbnail Options

1. Click the **Layer Option** icon located in the bottom-left corner of the **Layers** panel.

2. Choose **Thumbnail Options** from the fly-out menu that appears.

3. Select a size option from the **Thumbnail Options** fly-out submenu.

   IMPORTANT *To hide all thumbnails in the Layers panel, choose None from the Thumbnail Options fly-out submenu.*

4. To allow Expression Design to display pop-up thumbnails whenever the cursor hovers over a layer, choose **Popup Thumbnails.** A check mark is displayed next to the option in the submenu whenever it is enabled.

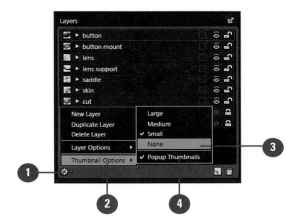

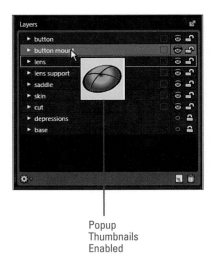

Popup
Thumbnails
Enabled

Drawing Shapes and Paths

8

Introduction

Although you can create pixel-based bitmap graphics in Expression Design, it is by nature a vector-drawing application. Vector graphics are not pixel based and therefore are not resolution dependent. Common graphic items such as icons, logos, and even animated characters can all be created in a vector-drawing application like Expression Design.

This chapter does not attempt to teach you how to draw. That's a skill that is either inherent in you, the artist, or acquired through years of training. However, this chapter does teach you how to apply your preexisting drawing skills in Expression Design using the various drawing tools.

The lessons that follow describe the differences between Bézier and B-spline paths and show you how to draw and edit both. The chapter also includes a full description of each node type: smooth, corner, and cusp.

In addition, this chapter walks you through every tool in the Pen toolset and explains how to edit paths using each one, including the Direct Selection tool and the Scissors tool. It also walks you through how to draw with the shape tools (Rectangle, Ellipse, and Polygon) and how to work with compound, clipping, and cloned paths. The last section explains how to import graphics that were created in Adobe Illustrator, and what to watch out for when you do.

Understanding Path Structure

In Expression Design, paths can be open (such as a simple line) or closed (such as a rectangle, ellipse, or polygon). Expression Design allows you to close an open path, join two open paths together (resulting in a shape), or split a closed path to make it open.

Every path and shape that you create in Expression Design is made up of straight and curved path segments that are held together by anchor points (called nodes). By moving or editing nodes, you can change the appearance of a shape or path.

There are two different types of curved path segments in Expression Design: Bézier ("beh-zee-ay") and B-spline.

Bézier Curves

Every node (or "point") along a Bézier path contains a set of control handles that determines the angle of the corresponding curve. There are three different types of Bézier nodes: smooth, unconstrained (cusp), and corner. Bézier curves are native to most other vector-drawing applications, such as Adobe Illustrator.

B-Spline Curves

The nodes along a B-spline path do not contain control handles like the Bézier nodes do. Instead, the angle of each curve is

determined by the position of each node along the path. In general, B-spline curves are much easier to control because they are more intuitive.

Path Direction

Every path, open or closed, contains a starting node and an ending node. (For closed paths, this is the same point.) When edges are made visible (which they are by default), Expression Design displays a red arrowhead over the ending node whenever you select the object.

The direction of the path affects the way certain stroke attributes, such as brush strokes, are displayed along the path or shape. You can reverse the direction of a path at any time, or when working with closed paths, you can change the starting node.

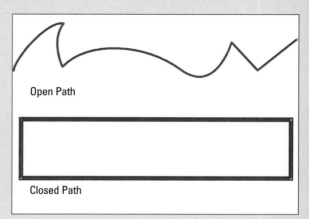

Open Path

Closed Path

Defining Bezier Curve Points

Every Bézier node contains two control handles: an "in" handle, which controls the angle of the curve leading into the anchor point; and an "out" handle, which controls the angle of the curve exiting the anchor point. You can recognize which handle controls the in or out curve by the direction that the path is facing.

There are three different types of Bézier points: smooth, corner, and unconstrained (cusp).

Smooth Points

When you create a smooth node with the Pen tool, both control handles are positioned opposite each other (180 degrees) and are symmetrical, which means that they are an equal distance from the anchor point. Moving one of the control handles with the Direct Selection tool results in the handles no longer being symmetrical; however, the curve remains smooth.

Corner Points

Corner points also contain two control handles that are fully retracted "inside" the anchor point. As a result, the path displays a sharp

corner rather than a smooth curve. You can access the hidden control handles using the Convert Anchor Point tool.

Unconstrained (Cusp) Points

Cusp points contain either one or two extended control handles, the latter of which can be positioned at any distance or angle from the anchor point.

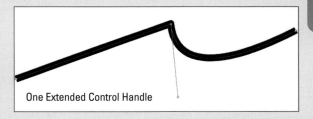

One Extended Control Handle

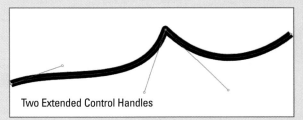

Two Extended Control Handles

Drawing with the Pen Tool

When learning how to use a vector-drawing application like Expression Design, an essential skill that you should master is drawing with the Pen tool. Although it might take a while to get the hang of it, this tedious yet very precise drawing tool offers you the most creative control. Your first steps are to learn how to create the three different types of anchor points (smooth, corner, and cusp) and to learn how to close a path.

Create a Smooth Point

1. Access the Pen tool by clicking its icon (the pen tip) in the **Tools** panel.

    IMPORTANT *If the Pen tool icon is not visible in the Tools panel, it is hidden behind one of the other tools in the Pen toolset. Click the current Pen toolset icon and hold down the mouse button to access the Pen tool from the fly-out menu.*

    TIMESAVER *Press P to access the Pen tool quickly.*

2. Click once on the artboard to create an initial anchor point.

3. Click and drag in any direction that you'd like the path to follow. Clicking creates a second anchor point; dragging causes the symmetrical control handles for the new point to appear. Continue to drag in any direction until the curve appears the way you like. Default fill and stroke attributes are not applied until you release the mouse button to complete the curve.

4. Repeat step 3 as many times as you like to add multiple curves to the path.

5. To end the open path, double-click or press **Enter** or **Esc**.

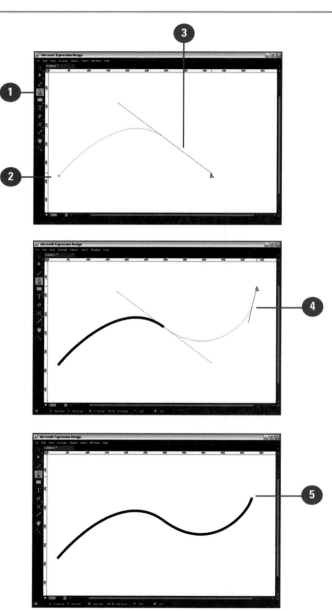

Create a Corner Point

1. Access the Pen tool by clicking its icon in the **Tools** panel or by pressing **P** on the keyboard.

2. Click once on the artboard to create an initial anchor point.

3. Click again in any direction that you'd like the path to follow. Default fill and stroke attributes are not applied until you release the mouse button to complete the path segment.

4. Repeat step 3 as many times as you like to add multiple corner points to the path.

5. To end the open path, double-click or press **Enter** or **Esc**.

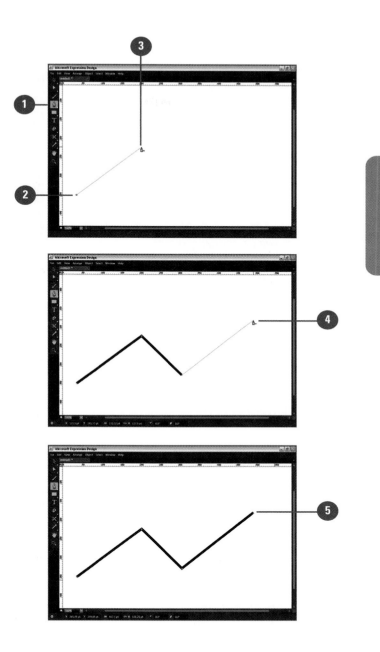

Create a Cusp Point

1. Access the Pen tool by clicking its icon in the **Tools** panel or by pressing **P** on the keyboard.

2. Click once on the artboard to create an initial anchor point.

3. To create a single-handle cusp point, with the in handle fully retracted, hold down **Ctrl+Alt** and click and drag.

   IMPORTANT *To create a cusp point with two control handles that work independently of each other, click and drag to create a smooth point with symmetrical handles. Before you release the mouse button, hold down Alt and drag one of the control handles in a different direction. Release the mouse button to complete the cusp point.*

   Default fill and stroke attributes are not applied until you release the mouse button.

4. Repeat step 3 as many times as you like to add multiple cusp points to the path.

5. To end the open path, double-click or press **Enter** or **Esc**.

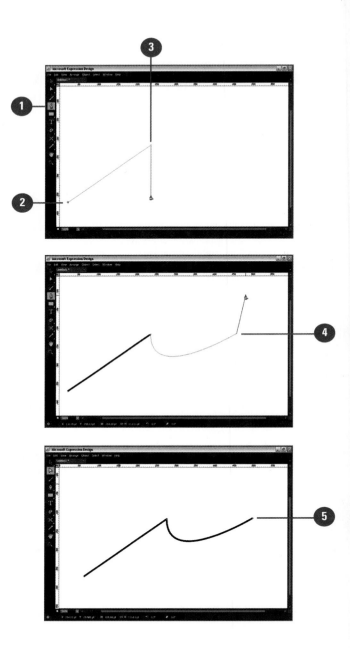

Create a Closed Path

1 Access the Pen tool by clicking its icon in the **Tools** panel or by pressing **P** on the keyboard.

2 Click once on the artboard to create an initial anchor point.

3 Create a path using a combination of smooth, corner, and cusp points.

4 Hover over the starting point of the path until you see a small circle icon appear next to the cursor.

5 When you see the Close Path icon next to the cursor, click to close the path. The starting point is converted into a corner point.

IMPORTANT *If the starting point was created by clicking and dragging (rather than just clicking), closing the path converts it into a cusp point with the in handle fully retracted and the out handle extended.*

You can also click and drag the starting point to create either a curve or cusp point (depending on the status of the starting point's out handle).

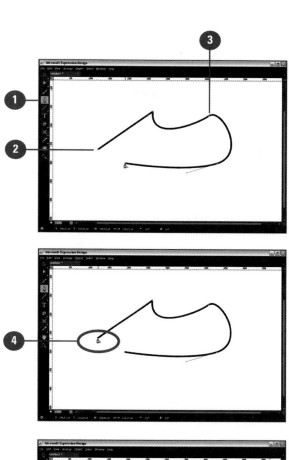

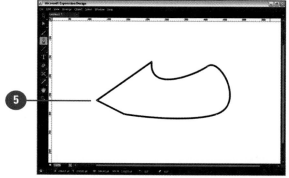

Editing Paths with the Direct Selection Tool

When it comes to drawing vector graphics in Expression Design, the Direct Selection tool works hand-in-hand with the Pen toolset. This is because the Direct Selection tool allows you to select individual or multiple anchor points and path segments. Doing so enables you to reposition (or even delete) points and segments to edit the appearance of a shape or path. You can also use the Direct Selection tool to move Bezier smooth and cusp node control handles, as well as B-spline nodes to edit curve angles.

Move Nodes and Path Segments

1. Access the Direct Selection tool by clicking its icon (the white arrow tip) in the **Tools** panel.

   IMPORTANT *If the Direct Selection tool icon is not visible in the Tools panel, it is hidden behind the Lasso Selection tool. Click and hold the Lasso Selection tool icon to access the Direct Selection tool from the fly-out menu.*

   TIMESAVER *Press A to access the Direct Selection tool quickly.*

2. Click directly on a node or path segment to select it. Expression Design displays a colored outline around the object after a node or path segment is selected. The outline color is determined by the layer the object currently resides on.

   When selecting a node, Expression Design fills the node with the currently assigned layer color. When selecting a path segment, Expression Design displays a small blue square at the exact point where you clicked along the path.

3. Drag the selected node or path segment to a new position on the artboard. Doing so changes the appearance of the shape or path.

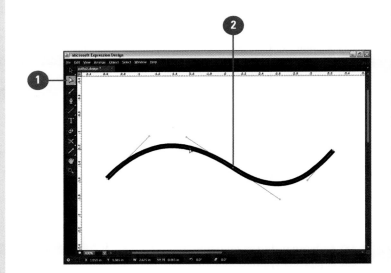

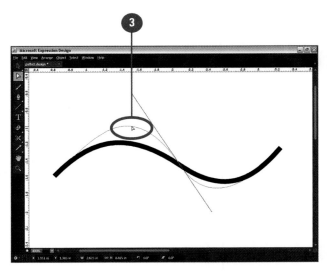

Move Smooth Point and Cusp Point Control Handles

① Access the Direct Selection tool by clicking its icon in the **Tools** panel or by pressing **A**.

② Click directly on a smooth or cusp point (or corresponding path segment) to select it. Expression Design displays the existing in and out control handles for each point at either end of the selected path segment.

③ Click and drag a control handle to change the angle of the curve.

Did You Know?

You can temporarily access the last used selection-making tool as you draw with the Pen tool. Rather than switching tools in the Tools panel, you can temporarily access the last used selection-making tool (Selection, Direct Selection, Lasso Selection, or Group Select) by holding down the Ctrl key.

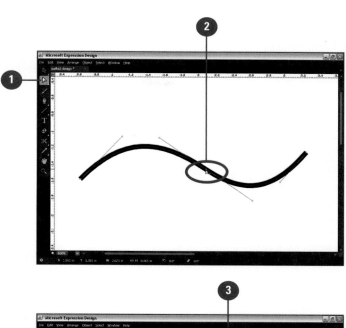

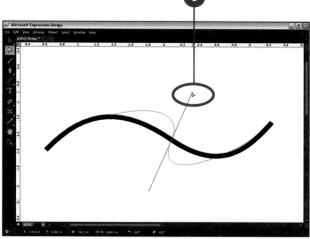

Select and Delete Nodes and Paths Segments

1 Access the Direct Selection tool by clicking its icon (the white arrow tip) in the **Tools** panel or by pressing **A**.

2 Click directly on a node or path segment to select it.

3 Press the **Delete** or **Backspace** key to remove the node and the corresponding path segments (positioned on either side of it) from the path.

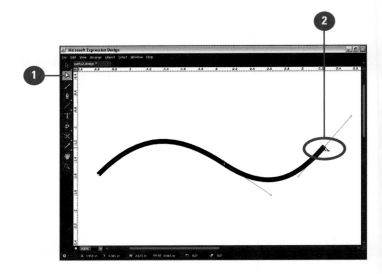

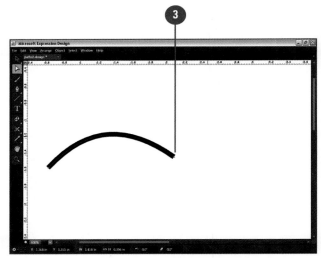

Editing Paths with the Pen Tools

The Pen toolset not only includes the Pen tool, but also the Add Anchor Point, Delete Anchor Point, and Convert Anchor Point tools. Together, these tools allow you to edit paths and shapes created with the Pen tool, in addition to those created with the B-Spline and Polyline tools.

Add Anchor Points

1 With a path already selected, access the Add Anchor Point tool by clicking its icon (the pen tip with a + next to it) in the **Tools** panel.

> **IMPORTANT** *If the Add Anchor Point tool icon is not visible in the Tools panel, it is hidden behind one of the other tools in the Pen toolset. Click the current Pen toolset icon and hold down the mouse button to access the Add Anchor Point tool from the fly-out menu.*

> **TIMESAVER** *Press = to access the Add Anchor Point tool quickly.*

2 Hover over any path segment until the cursor changes from white to black.

3 When the cursor changes, click to add an anchor point.

> ### Did You Know?
>
> ***You can temporarily access the Add Anchor Point tool as you draw with the Pen tool.*** Rather than switching tools in the Tools panel, you can temporarily access the Add Anchor Point tool by simply hovering the Pen tool cursor over any path segment.

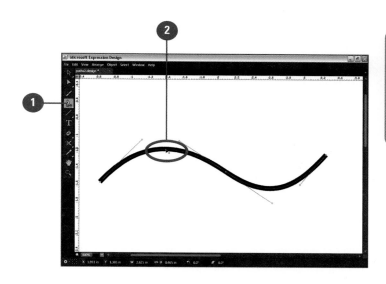

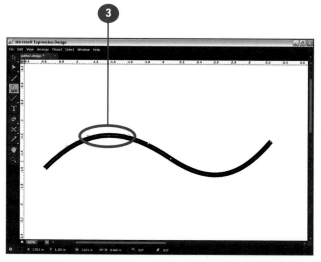

Delete Anchor Points

1. With a path already selected, access the Delete Anchor Point tool by clicking its icon (the pen tip with a - next to it) in the **Tools** panel.

   IMPORTANT *If the Delete Anchor Point tool icon is not visible in the Tools panel, it is hidden behind one of the other tools in the Pen toolset. Click the current Pen toolset icon and hold down the mouse button to access the Delete Anchor Point tool from the fly-out menu.*

   TIMESAVER *Press - to access the Delete Anchor Point tool quickly.*

2. Hover over any node until the cursor changes from white to black.

3. When the cursor changes, click to delete the anchor point.

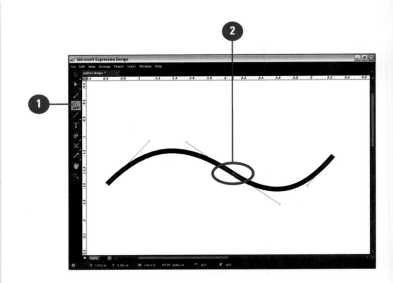

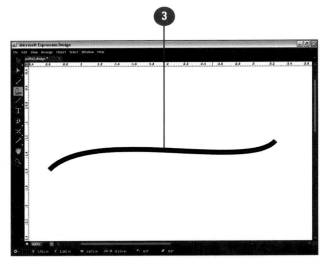

Did You Know?

You can temporarily access the Delete Anchor Point tool as you draw with the Pen tool. Rather than switching tools in the Tools panel, you can temporarily access the Delete Anchor Point tool by simply hovering the Pen tool cursor over any node along a path.

Convert Anchor Points

1 With a path already selected, access the Convert Anchor Point tool by clicking its icon in the **Tools** panel.

IMPORTANT *If the Convert Anchor Point tool icon is not visible in the Tools panel, it is hidden behind one of the other tools in the Pen toolset. Click the current Pen toolset icon and hold down the mouse button to access the Convert Anchor Point tool from the fly-out menu.*

TIMESAVER *Press Shift+C to access the Convert Anchor Point tool quickly.*

2 Hover over any node until you see a small node icon appear next to the cursor.

3 When the cursor changes, click and drag the point to access its symmetrical control handles.

Did You Know?

You can temporarily access the Convert Anchor Point tool as you draw with the Pen tool. Rather than switching tools in the Tools panel, you can temporarily access the Convert Anchor Point tool by holding down the Alt key.

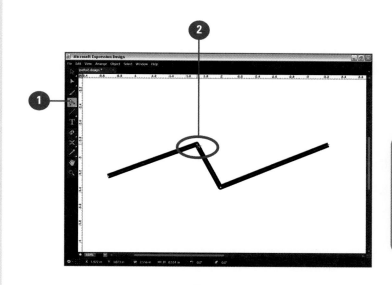

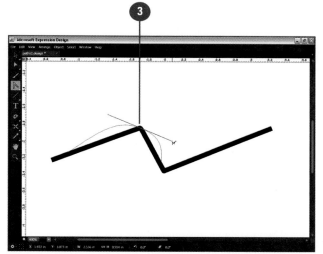

Drawing with the B-Spline Tool

The B-Spline tool is a nice alternative to the Pen tool, mostly because it allows you to create intricate curves without ever having to move any node control handles or create any cusp points. But you can also use both tools together by adding B-spline paths to Bezier paths and vice-versa. For example, if you are the type of designer who prefers the precision of the Pen tool but still has difficulty drawing or tracing intricate Bézier curves, you can always switch to the B-Spline tool to make things a little easier.

Create a Smooth Point

① Access the B-Spline tool by clicking its icon in the **Tools** panel.

IMPORTANT *If the B-Spline tool icon is not visible in the Tools panel, it is hidden behind one of the other tools in the Pen toolset. Click the current Pen toolset icon and hold down the mouse button to access the B-spline tool from the fly-out menu.*

TIMESAVER *Press **W** to access the B-Spline tool quickly.*

② Click once on the artboard to create an initial anchor point.

③ Move the cursor in any direction that you'd like the path to follow, and then click and drag to create a smooth point.

④ Repeat step 3 as many times as you like to add multiple curves to the path.

⑤ To end the open path, double-click or press **Enter** or **Esc**.

Default fill and stroke attributes are not applied until you end the path.

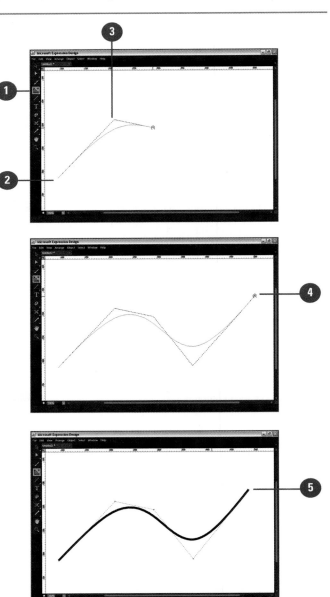

Create a Corner Point

1. Access the B-Spline tool by clicking its icon in the **Tools** panel or by pressing **W** on the keyboard.

2. Click once on the artboard to create an initial anchor point.

3. Move the cursor in any direction that you'd like the path to follow, and Alt+click to create a corner point.

4. Repeat step 3 as many times as you like to add multiple corner points to the path.

5. To end the open path, double-click or press **Enter** or **Esc**. Default fill and stroke attributes are not applied until you end the path.

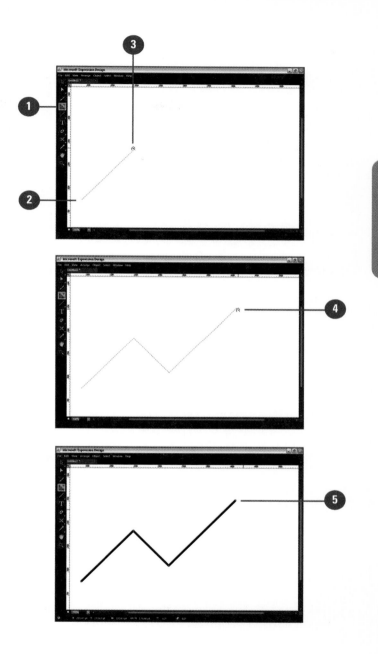

Create a Closed Path

1. Access the B-Spline tool by clicking its icon in the **Tools** panel or by pressing **W** on the keyboard.

2. Click once on the artboard to create an initial anchor point.

3. Create a path using a combination of smooth and corner points.

4. Hover over the starting point of the path. Expression Design displays a preview of what the path will look like when it is closed.

5. When you see the preview, click to close the path. Default fill and stroke attributes are not applied until you close the path.

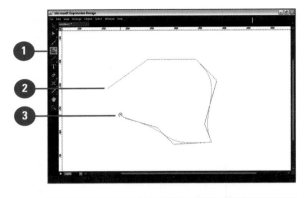

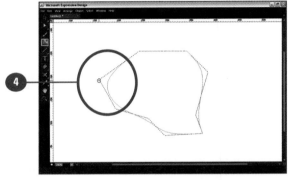

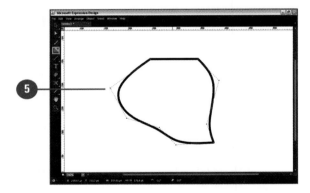

Drawing with the Polyline Tool

Combine Straight Lines with Circular Arcs

1 Access the Polyline tool by clicking its icon in the **Tools** panel.

> **IMPORTANT** *If the Polyline tool icon is not visible in the Tools panel, it is hidden behind one of the other tools in the Pen toolset. Click the current Pen toolset icon and hold down the mouse button to access the Polyline tool from the fly-out menu.*

2 Click once on the artboard to create an initial anchor point.

3 Move the cursor to create a straight line segment in any direction that you'd like the path to follow. Hold down **Shift** to constrain the angle to 45-degree increments. Click again to create a second anchor point.

4 Move the cursor away from the last anchor point and click and drag to create a circular arc. The size of the arc is determined by how far you move the mouse cursor before clicking and dragging.

5 Click again to end the circular arc. Move the cursor to create another straight line segment.

6 To end the open path, double-click or press **Enter** or **Esc**. Default fill and stroke attributes are not applied until you end the path.

If you've ever tried to draw a circular arc in the middle of a straight line segment with the Pen tool, you know how difficult it can be. Thankfully, Expression Design has provided a Polyline tool that allows you to complete this task using Bezier curves, but without ever having to move a single control handle.

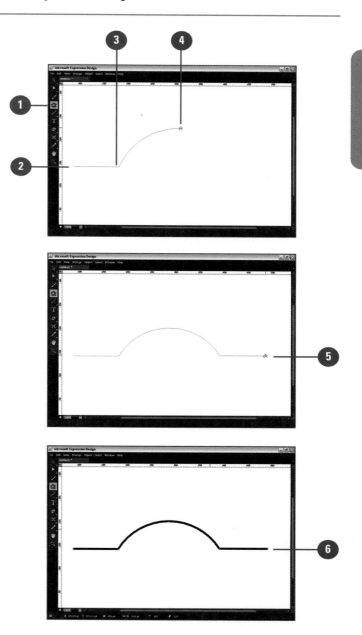

Splitting Paths

You can use the Scissors tool to separate open or closed paths by clicking on any path segment, Bézier node, or B-spline corner node. This can be extremely useful when creating vector graphics. For example, one quick and easy way to create a perfect half circle is to draw a circle with the Ellipse tool and cut it in half with the Scissors tool.

Cut the Path with the Scissors Tool

1. Access the Scissors tool by clicking its icon in the **Tools** panel.

   IMPORTANT *If the Scissors tool icon is not visible in the Tools panel, it is hidden behind one of the other tools in the toolset. Click the current toolset icon and hold down the mouse button to access the Scissors tool from the fly-out menu.*

   TIMESAVER *Press C to access the Scissors tool quickly.*

2. Click anywhere along the path to select it.

3. Click any path segment, any Bézier node, or any B-spline corner node (not B-spline curve nodes) to split the path. Doing so creates two new anchor points: one end point and one start point.

   IMPORTANT *When you split a B-spline curve by clicking its path segment (not the off-path node), Expression Design automatically converts the B-spline paths into Bézier paths.*

4. Access the Selection tool by clicking its icon in the **Tools** panel or by pressing **V**.

5. Select either path and reposition it on the artboard.

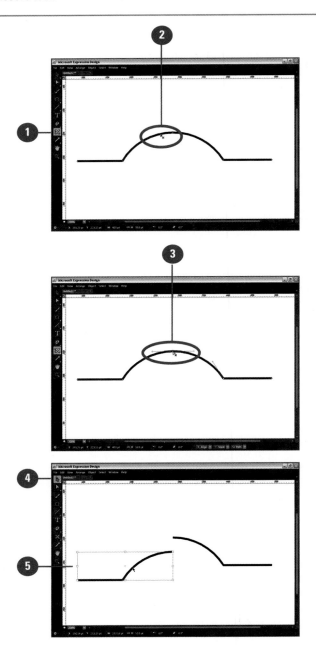

Drawing with the Rectangle Tool

Although it is entirely possible to draw a rectangle using the Pen tool or B-Spline tool, it is much quicker and easier to do so using the Rectangle tool—not to mention that by using the Rectangle tool, you can create rounded corners by entering a simple setting into the Properties panel, as opposed to manipulating multiple nodes and control handles with the Pen toolset or B-Spline tool.

Create a Rectangle

1 Access the Rectangle tool by clicking its icon in the **Tools** panel.

> **IMPORTANT** *If the Rectangle tool icon is not visible in the Tools panel, it is hidden behind one of the other tools in the shape toolset. Click the current shape toolset icon and hold down the mouse button to access the Rectangle tool from the fly-out menu.*

> **TIMESAVER** *Press M to access the Rectangle tool quickly.*

2 Click and drag to create a rectangle.

3 Release the mouse button when the rectangle appears the way you like. Default fill and stroke attributes are not applied until you release the mouse button.

> **TIMESAVER** *To create a perfect square, hold down Shift as you click and drag with the Rectangle tool.*

> **TIMESAVER** *To draw a rectangle from the center outward, hold down Alt as you click and drag with the Rectangle tool.*

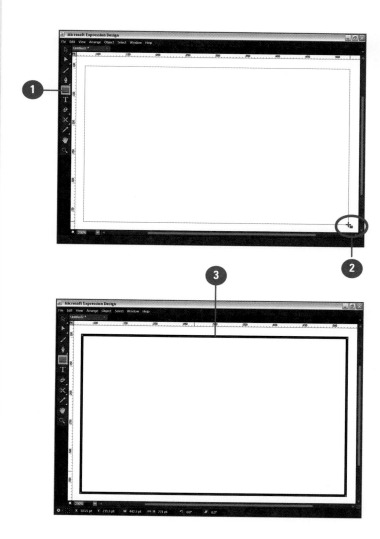

Create Rounded Corners

1 Select a rectangle (or multiple rectangles) in the document.

2 In the **Properties** panel, enter a new value in the **Corner Radius** field of the **Edit Rectangle** pane.

3 Expression Design automatically updates the selected rectangle(s) in the document.

Did You Know?

Using the drawing tools to edit a shape that was created with the shape tools causes you to lose the ability to apply shape properties to it. If you use the Pen toolset and Direct Selection tools to edit a shape drawn with any of the shape tools, you forfeit the ability to apply shape properties to it. After the shape is edited, the Edit pane automatically disappears from the Properties panel. Any shape properties applied to the shape before editing it with the drawing tools remain intact but can no longer be edited using the settings in the Properties panel.

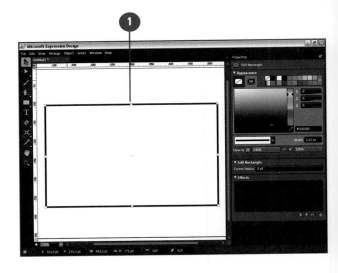

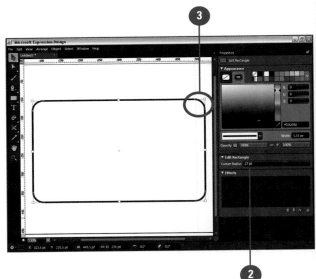

Drawing with the Ellipse Tool

As it is with the Rectangle tool, the Ellipse tool makes it much easier to create this basic shape without having to resort to manipulating multiple nodes and control handles. With the Ellipse tool, you can create an oval (or even a perfect circle) by simply clicking and dragging.

Create an Ellipse

1 Access the Ellipse tool by clicking its icon in the **Tools** panel.

> **IMPORTANT** *If the Ellipse tool icon is not visible in the Tools panel, it is hidden behind one of the other tools in the shape toolset. Click the current shape toolset icon and hold down the mouse button to access the Ellipse tool from the fly-out menu.*

> **TIMESAVER** *Press L to access the Ellipse tool quickly.*

2 Click and drag to create a new ellipse.

3 Release the mouse button when the ellipse appears the way you like. Default fill and stroke attributes are not applied until you release the mouse button.

> **TIMESAVER** *To create a perfect circle, hold down Shift as you click and drag with the Ellipse tool.*

> **TIMESAVER** *To draw an ellipse from the center outward, hold down Alt as you click and drag with the Ellipse tool.*

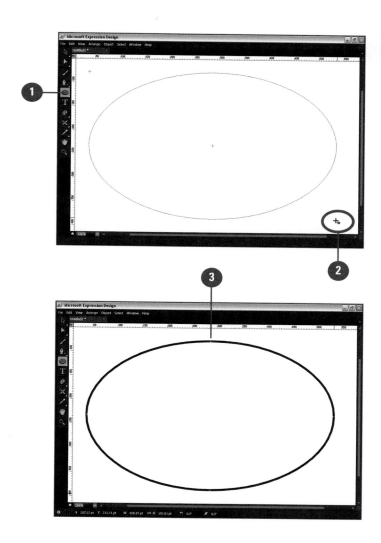

Drawing with the Polygon Tool

The Polygon tool allows you to create multisided shapes, stars, and bursts. All you need to do is enter the number of points that you'd like to include in the Create Polygon pane of the Properties panel and then click and drag with the tool. An Inner Depth setting allows you to specify how far inward the points should appear, and a Twirl angle setting allows you to apply a twirl percentage to the extended points of the shape. As long as you do not edit the polygon with the Pen toolset or Direct Selection tool, you can change these settings at any time. Doing so allows you to edit the path without using any tedious drawing tools.

Create a Polygon

1 Access the Polygon tool by clicking its icon in the **Tools** panel.

IMPORTANT *If the Polygon tool icon is not visible in the Tools panel, it is hidden behind one of the other tools in the shape toolset. Click the current shape toolset icon and hold down the mouse button to access the Polygon tool from the fly-out menu.*

TIMESAVER *Press J to access the Polygon tool quickly.*

2 Enter the number of points and the preferred **Inner Depth** and **Twirl Angle** percentages in the **Create Polygon** pane of the **Properties** panel. These settings become the new default values for any new polygons you create.

3 Click and drag to create a new polygon.

4 Release the mouse button when the polygon appears the way you like. Default fill and stroke attributes are not applied until you release the mouse button.

> **Did You Know?**
>
> ***By default, the Polygon tool always draws from the center outward.*** Unlike drawing with the Rectangle and Ellipse tools, it is not necessary to hold down Alt to draw from the center outward with the Polygon tool.

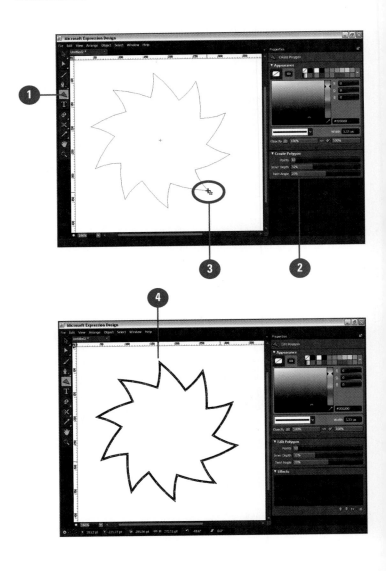

Creating a Compound Path

From time to time, you might need to create a shape that contains a "hole" in it, which allows you to see through to the underlying graphics. A traditional doughnut or bagel shape are prime examples. In Expression Design, you can create this type of shape by combining two separate overlapping shapes into a compound path.

Apply the Make Compound Path Command

1. In a new document, click the **Fill** icon in the **Appearance** pane of the **Properties** panel. Choose a new default fill color using any one of the following methods:

    ◆ Using the color picker

    ◆ Entering RGB or hex values

    ◆ Clicking a saved color swatch

2. Access the Ellipse tool by clicking its icon in the **Tools** panel or by pressing **L**.

3. Shift+click and drag to create a perfect circle.

4. Choose **Copy** from the **Edit** menu, and then choose **Paste in Front** from the **Edit** menu.

5. Repeat step 1 to choose a different fill color in the Properties panel.

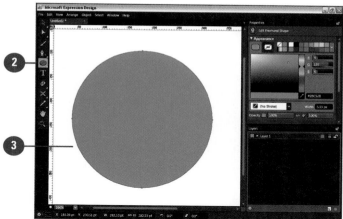

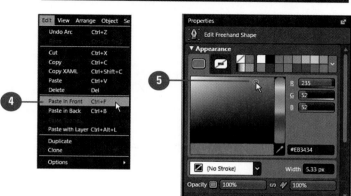

6. In the Action bar, make sure the Registration Point is centered and the Width and Height settings are linked. Enter a much lower Width or Height setting to reduce the size of the topmost circle.

7. Choose **All** from the **Select** menu, or press **Ctrl+A**.

8. Under the **Object** menu, choose **Make Compound Path** from the fly-out submenu, or press **Ctrl+8**.

Expression Design combines the two images into a compound path.

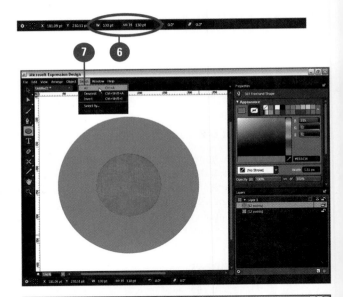

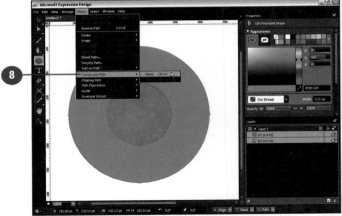

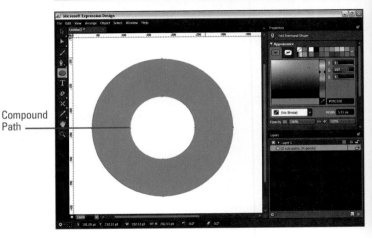

Compound Path

Releasing a Compound Path

Unlike applying Path Operations (see Chapter 12, "Transforming Objects"), working with compound paths allows you to preserve the original shapes that make up the path and release the effect at any time. However, you should be aware that releasing a compound path does not return the respective shapes to their original states.

Apply the Release Compound Path Command

① Select any compound path object in the document.

② Under the **Object** menu, choose **Release** from the **Compound Path** fly-out submenu.

> **TIMESAVER** *Press Ctrl+Shift+8 to apply the Release Compound Path command quickly.*

The attributes that were previously applied to the top object prior to creating the compound path are not automatically reapplied. Instead, the top object inherits the fill and stroke attributes of the bottom object.

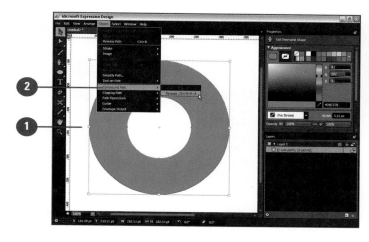

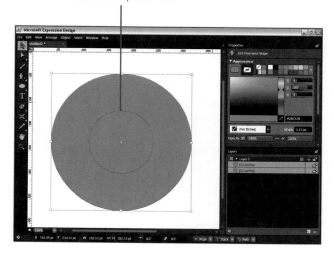

Released Compound Path

Cloning Paths

Expression Design is unique in that it gives you the ability to work with cloned paths. This feature allows you to create duplicates of a specific object and then apply shape edits globally. This means that any edits made to the source object using the Pen toolset or Direct Selction tool are also applied to the corresponding clones.

Apply the Clone Command

① Select any path or shape in the document that you'd like to use as a source object.

② Choose **Clone** from the **Edit** menu.

③ The cloned duplicate appears at the top of the layer stack. Reposition the object on the artboard.

④ Edit the source object using any of the drawing tools, such as the Pen toolset and Direct Selection tool. (Resizing with the Selection tool has no effect.) Any changes that you apply to the shape of the source object with these tools are also applied to the clone.

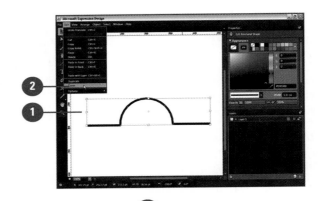

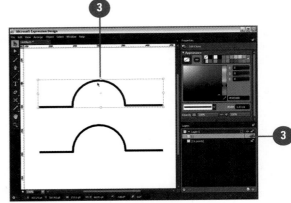

Edits to Original Object Are Applied to Clone Automatically

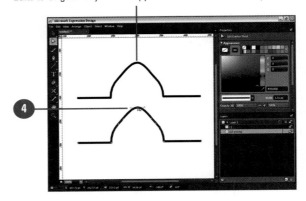

Did You Know?

You can clone a compound path.
Expression Design allows you to clone a compound path; however, releasing the path on the source object has no effect on its clone.

You can clone a grouped object.
Expression Design allows you to clone a grouped object; however, ungrouping the source object or repositioning objects within the group have no effect on its clone.

You cannot clone a text object.
Expression Design does not allow you to clone a text object unless it is converted into a path first.

Creating a Clipping Path

In Expression Design, a clipping path is a type of vector mask that allows you to mask one object inside of another. This is a commonly used technique for applying background patterns. Masked objects can be selected and transformed from within the clipping group. You can also release the clipping mask at any time.

Apply the Clipping Path Commands

1. Select two different objects that are positioned on the same layer and arrange them so that they are overlapping each other.

2. Select both objects with the Selection tool.

3. Under the **Object** menu, choose **Make with Bottom Path** or **Make with Top Path** from the **Clipping Path** submenu. Doing so masks one object (top or bottom) inside of the other. Expression Design automatically groups the masked objects in the Layers panel and names the group [Clipping Mask].

The selected objects are combined into a clipping mask.

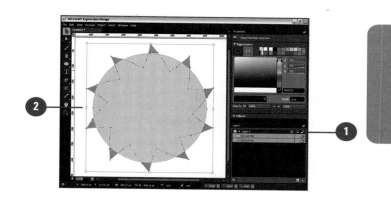

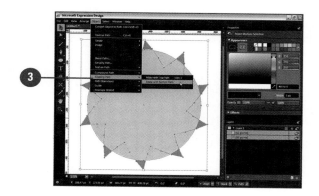

Clipping Mask

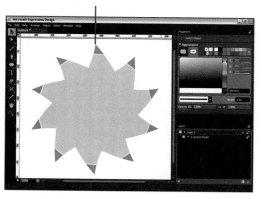

Did You Know?

You can include grouped objects and text objects in a clipping path. Expression Design allows you to mask a grouped object or a text object inside of an underlying shape.

You can release a clipping mask at anytime. To release the mask, select the object, then point to the Object menu, and choose Release from the Clipping Path submenu.

Importing Adobe Illustrator Graphics

Adobe Illustrator is a vector-drawing application, similar to Expression Design, that is commonly used by creative professionals. If you're familiar with Illustrator, you might have some preexisting Illustrator graphics that you'd like to use in Expression Design, or you might receive one from a third-party source, such as a freelance designer who is contributing to your project. You can import Illustrator graphics; however, some of the features available in Illustrator might not translate well in Expression Design, such as 3D effects, transparencies, and various other appearance attributes. As a general rule, the simpler the graphic is in Illustrator, the better your chances are of importing it successfully in Expression Design.

Apply the Import Command

1. In a new document, choose **Import** from the **File** menu.

   TIMESAVER *Press Ctrl+I to quickly apply the Import command.*

2. In the Import Document dialog box that appears, make sure that **All Supported Formats** is chosen in the **Files of Type** field, and browse to the Adobe Illustrator file (.ai) on your system.

3. Click **Open** to import the Adobe Illustrator graphic into your Expression Design document.

   Expression design places the imported graphic in a new layer above Layer 1 in the Layers panel.

> ### Did You Know?
>
> **You can import Adobe Illustrator files, but you can't export them.** Expression Design allows you to import Adobe Illustrator files, but it does not allow you to export your graphics in the .ai format.

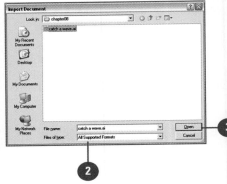

Imported Graphic

Applying Fills, Strokes, and Effects

Introduction

Learning to apply fills, strokes, and effects is an essential part of learning to create graphics in Expression Design. To apply color to your artwork, you must do so by applying it to a fill or stroke. Live effects allow you to add dimension and a sense of realism to your graphics in the form of editable drop shadows, outer glows, and bevels (just to name a few). In fact, it's safe to say that without the ability to apply any fills, strokes, or effects, your graphics would be pretty boring. Thankfully, Expression Design does include these attribute features and makes working with them easy and fun.

This chapter walks you through the process of choosing specific stroke properties such as width, color, and joint and cap settings. It also shows you how to create a dashed stroke and apply a dash pattern. It also takes you on a guided tour through the Brush Gallery explains how to create a custom brushstroke, and shows you how to use the Paintbrush tool to simulate traditional media, such as oils and watercolors.

In addition, this chapter shows how to apply solid color fills, gradient fills, and image fills to selected objects. You will also learn how to transform image fills and gradients using the Fill Transform and Gradient Transform tools.

Finally, you will learn how to apply and edit live effects in Expression Design and copy attributes using the Color Dropper and Attribute Dropper.

What You'll Do

Apply Stroke Width and Color Attributes

Change Stroke Joints and Caps

Create a Dashed Stroke

Use the Brush Gallery

Create a Custom Brushstroke

Work with the Paintbrush Tool

Reverse Path Direction

Apply Fill Color

Apply Image Fills

Transform Image Fills

Change Fill and Stroke Opacity

Apply Blend Modes

Apply Gradients to Strokes and Fills

Transform Gradients

Apply Live Effects

Copy Attributes

Applying Stroke Width and Color Attributes

Giving you the ability to apply a stroke to an object is considered standard fare for a drawing application, and Expression Design is no exception. In Expression Design you can apply strokes to shapes, lines, open paths, and editable text objects, but not to imported bitmap images.

Enter New Stroke Appearance Settings

1 Select any shape, line, open path, or editable text object in the document.

2 In the **Appearance** pane of the **Properties** panel, enter a different value into the **Width** field.

3 Also in the **Appearance** pane of the **Properties** panel, click the **Stroke** icon to bring it to the front.

4 Choose a new stroke color using any one of the following methods:

 ◆ Using the color picker

 ◆ Entering RGB or hex values

 ◆ Clicking a saved color swatch

The new stroke attributes are updated in the document as you enter the new settings.

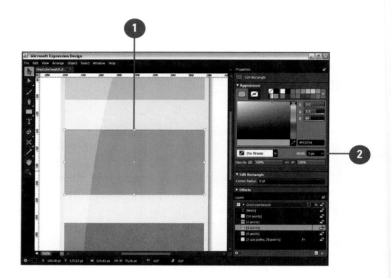

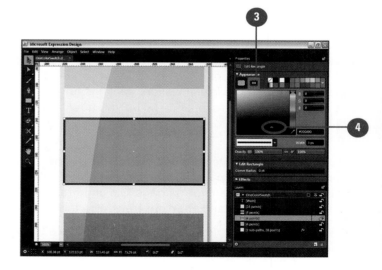

Changing Stroke Joints and Caps

Expression Design allows you to control the stroke appearance for all corner points and the starting and ending points of an open path, no matter whether the path is made up of Bezier or B-spline points. You can access the Joint and Cap settings by revealing the advanced properties section of the Appearance pane in the Properties panel. Note that these settings do not apply to strokes that are applied to editable text objects.

Choose Join Properties

1 Select any shape, line, or open path in the document.

2 Click the **Advanced Settings** icon (the down arrow) at the bottom of the **Appearance** pane in the **Properties** panel to access the Stroke properties.

3 Choose a join setting from the **Joint** pop-up list. The setting that you choose affects the way all corner and cusp points appear in the document:

◆ **Miter Join** creates a pointed edge where the two path segments meet.

◆ **Bevel Join** creates a beveled edge where the two path segments meet.

◆ **Round Join** creates a rounded edge where the two path segments meet.

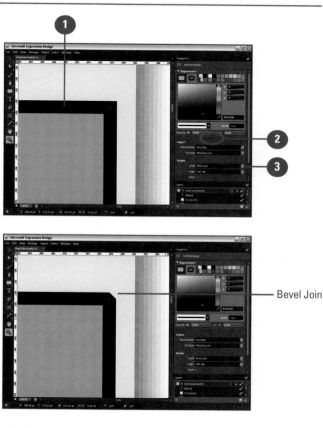

Bevel Join

Round Join

Choose Cap Properties

① Select any line or open path in the document.

② Click the **Advanced Settings** icon (the down arrow) at the bottom of the **Properties** panel to access the Stroke properties.

③ Choose a cap setting from the **Caps** pop-up list. The setting that you choose affects the way all selected open path start and end points appear in the document:

◆ **Flat Cap** adds a flat edge without extending the stroke past the start or end point.

◆ **Round Cap** adds a round edge and extends the stroke past the start or end point.

◆ **Square Cap** adds a flat edge and extends the stroke past the start or end point.

Did You Know?

Enabling the Break at Joints option changes the way a stroke appears across corner points. When you a apply a stroke with this option disabled, the stroke is either stretched or repeated across the entire length of the path. When it is enabled, it forces the stroke to start and stop at each corner point, which can result in corners appearing uneven.

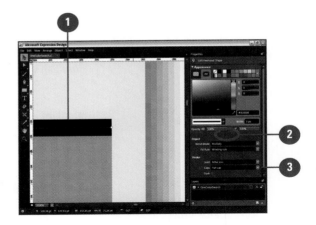

Round Cap

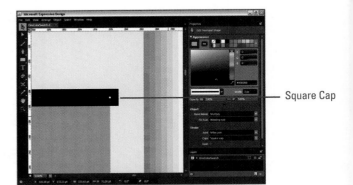

Square Cap

Creating a Dashed Stroke

With a simple click of a button, you can create a dashed stroke in Expression Design. You can specify the amount of space to use for every dash and gap along the path or create a dash pattern by entering multiple values in the Dash field.

Enable the Dashed Stroke Option

1 Select any shape, line, or open path in the document and apply a stroke to it.

2 Click the **Advanced Settings** icon (the down arrow) at the bottom of the **Appearance** pane in the **Properties** panel to access the Stroke properties.

3 Enable the dash option. In the dynamic field that appears, enter the preferred amount of space (in points) that you'd like to appear between dashes.

If you enter a single number into the Dash field, Expression Design applies the value to both the dash and the gap.

4 Enter two or more numbers into the dash field to create a dash pattern. For example, if you enter 12 24 36, Expression Design creates a 12-point dash, followed by a 24-point gap, followed by a 36-point dash, followed by a 12-point gap, and so on.

Did You Know?

You cannot add a dashed stroke to editable text. Although you can add a stroke to editable text, you cannot make it dashed.

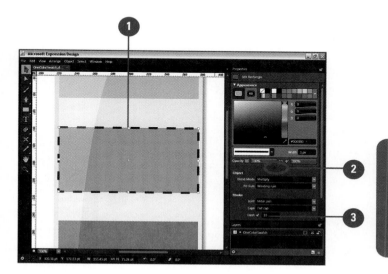

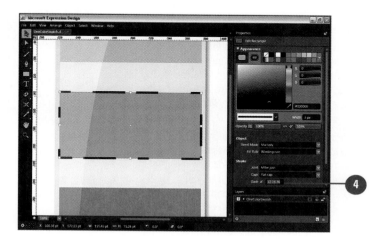

Using the Brush Gallery

The Brush Gallery, accessible via the Appearance pane of the Properties panel, contains a virtual treasure trove of creative strokes that can be applied to preexisting shapes or applied directly to the canvas with the Paithbrush tool. Many of these brushes simulate natural media, such as those found in the Oils, Acrylic, and Watercolors categories.

Select a Brush from the Gallery List

① In the **Appearance** pane of the **Properties** panel, click the down-facing arrow next to the currently selected brushstroke. Doing so reveals the the Brush Gallery pop-up list.

② Select a brush from the **Favorites** list, the **Most Recent** list, or from any of the available categories in the **Categories** list.

IMPORTANT *To access the brushes contained within a certain category (such as Acrylic, Ink, or Oils), click the toggle arrow next to the category's name in the list.*

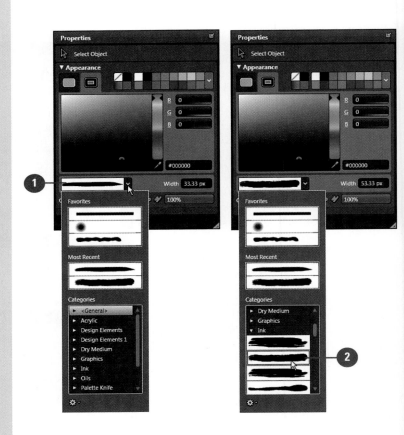

Creating a Custom Brushstroke

You can use the drawing tools to create a custom brush from scratch or edit an existing brush from the gallery. Expression Design also contains a special set of brush-editing tools that are only accessible through the edit window for the stroke. With these tools, you can control the width and starting point for the stroke in addition to anchoring and repeating specific shapes along the stroke's pattern.

Redefine a Brushstroke Using the Drawing Tools

1 From the Brush Gallery, select a brush from the **Favorites** list, the **Most Recent** list, or from any of the available categories in the **Categories** list.

2 In the bottom-left corner of the Brush Gallery window, choose **Edit Stroke** from the **Stroke Options** pop-up list, or choose **Edit Stroke Definition** from the **Stroke** fly-out submenu, accessible under the **Object** menu.

3 Expression Design opens a new document window for the stroke. Edit the stroke using any of the path-editing tools, such as the Pen toolset, Scissors, or Direct Selection tool. You can also resize the stroke with the Selection tool and apply a different fill color.

4 Choose **Close** from the **File** menu, or click the Stroke Definition window's close button in the Flip bar.

5 In the Save Stroke dialog box that appears, enter a stroke name and default width (in points). Choose the category where you'd like to save the stroke and click **OK**.

The new brush is added to the Brush Gallery.

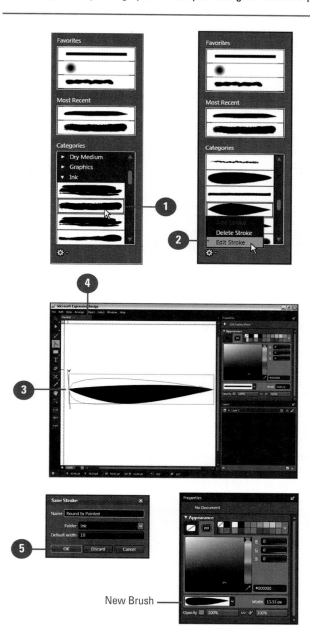

New Brush

Create a New Stroke Definition

1. In a new document window, create a brush stroke using any of the drawing tools, such as the Pen toolset, the shape tools, or the Direct Selection tool.

2. Select all the objects that you would like to include in the brush stroke.

3. In the bottom-left corner of the Brush Gallery window, choose **Add Stroke** from the **Stroke Options** pop-up list, or choose **New Stroke Definition** from the **Stroke** fly-out submenu, accessible under the **Object** menu.

4. Expression Design opens a new document window for the stroke. If necessary, make any additional edits to the stroke using the tools that are only available in this window (the Stroke Definition Box, Anchor Point, and Repeat tools).

5. Click **OK** to close and save the edited brush as described previously in the "Redefine a Brushstroke Using the Drawing Tools" task.

   The new brush is added to the Brush Gallery.

Did You Know?

The Default Width setting is only instated when you apply the stroke to a path that has no Width value applied. When you apply the stroke to a path that has no Width value applied, Expression Design defers to the stroke's Default Width setting.

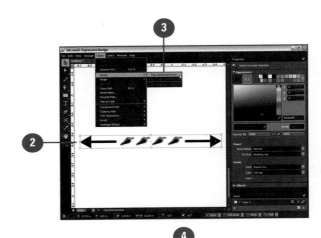

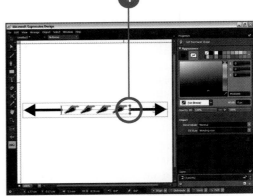

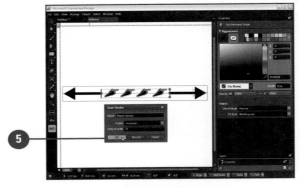

New Brush

Reposition the Stroke Definition Box

1. Access a selected stroke's edit window as described previously in the "Redefine a Brushstroke Using the Drawing Tools" task. A red box with a horizontal arrow surrounds the stroke. This is called the stroke definition box.

2. Select the **Stroke Definition Box** tool and redefine the edges of the existing box by dragging over the stroke diagonally. Doing so redefines the width and starting position of the stroke.

   The position of the arrowhead determines how far offset the stroke will be to the starting point of the path when you apply the stroke. The height of the stroke definition box determines the thickness (or width) of the stroke when it is applied.

3. Click **OK** to close and save the edited brush as described in the "Redefine a Brushstroke Using the Drawing Tools" task.

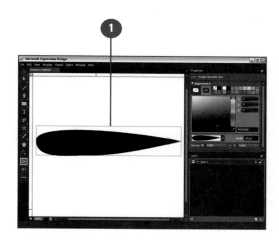

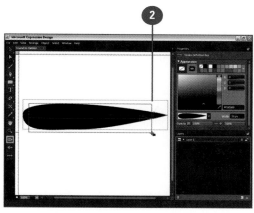

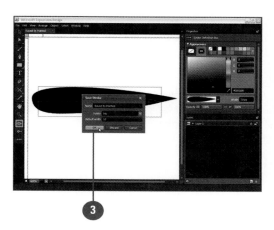

Anchor Nodes

1 Access a selected stroke's edit window as described in the "Redefine a Brushstroke Using the Drawing Tools" task.

2 Using the Direct Selection or Lasso Selection tool, select the path nodes that you want to anchor. Then right-click and choose one of the following options from the context menu:

◆ **Anchor To Start** anchors the nodes to the path's starting point.

◆ **Anchor to End** anchors the nodes to the path's ending point.

3 If you'd like to anchor the nodes to an arbitrary point along the path, select the **Anchor Point** tool and drag the anchor marker along the red arrow to the preferred position.

4 Close and save the edited brush as described in "Redefine a Brushstroke Using the Drawing Tools."

The stroke is updated wherever it is applied in the document.

See Also

See Chapter 5,"Making Selections," for a refresher on how to select individual nodes along a path with the Direct Selection tool.

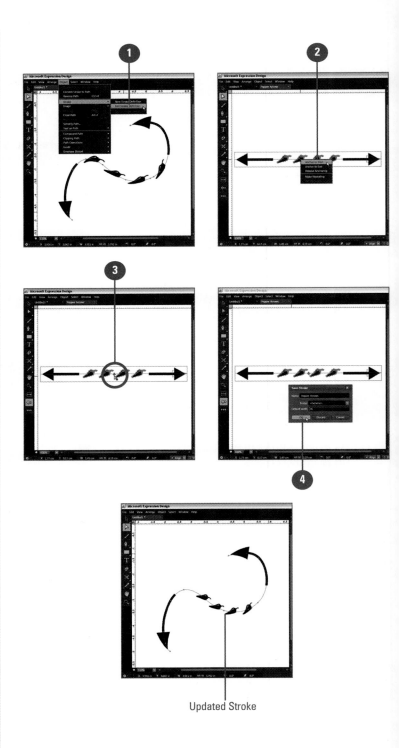

Updated Stroke

Repeat Shapes

1. Access a selected stroke's edit window as described in the "Redefine a Brushstroke Using the Drawing Tools" task.

2. Select the shape you want to repeat. Then right-click and choose **Make Repeating** from the context menu.

3. Expression Design automatically switches to the Repeat tool and displays a pair of repeat handles at either end of the path's stroke definition box. You can control which areas of the path repeat (and how often) by dragging the repeat handles in with the tool.

4. Close and save the edited brush as described in the "Redefine a Brushstroke Using the Drawing Tools" task.

   The stroke is updated wherever it is applied in the document.

Did You Know?

Expression Design allows you to anchor repeat handles. To anchor a repeat handle, press and hold Shift and click the handle with the Repeat tool. When the first repeat handle is anchored, the repeating pattern always starts at the beginning of the destination path. When the second repeat handle is anchored, the pattern always ends at the end of the path.

It is possible to adjust the height of repeating shapes. To adjust how large the repeating shape will be at the end of the pattern, drag the second repeat handle's up or down arrow icons. Dragging out (away from the red arrow) increases height along the path; dragging in (towards the red arrow) decreases height.

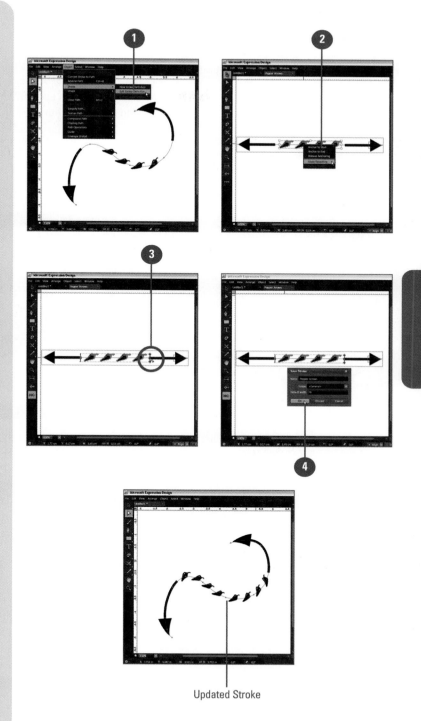

Updated Stroke

Working with the Paintbrush Tool

The Paintbrush tool allows you to create freehand shapes and paths. It also allows you to simulate traditional media, such as oils and watercolors, by using it with the natural media brushes available in the Brush Gallery. As you paint with the Paintbrush tool, Expression Design converts each freehand stroke into a Bézier path that can also be edited with the Pen toolset and Direct Selection tool.

Create Freehand Shapes and Paths

1. Click the **Paintbrush** tool icon (the paintbrush) in the **Tools** panel.

    TIMESAVER *Press B to access the Paintbrush tool quickly.*

2. From the Brush Gallery, select a brush from the **Favorites** list, the **Most Recent** list, or from any of the available categories in the **Categories** list.

3. In the **Appearance** pane of the **Properties** panel, enter a value into the **Width** field.

4. Also in the **Appearance** pane of the **Properties** panel, click the **Stroke** icon to bring it to the front. Choose a new stroke color.

5. Click and drag in any direction to create a freehand path or shape. Expression Design automatically adds Bézier nodes to the path as you draw.

    When you release the mouse button, Expression Design automatically selects the path and displays the nodes.

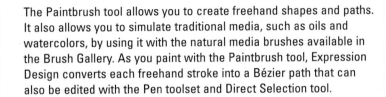

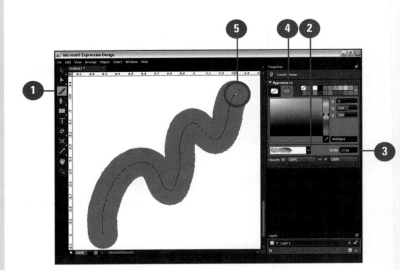

Bézier Path

Reversing Path Direction

Every path, open or closed, contains a starting node and an ending node. (For closed paths, this is the same point.) When edges are made visible (which they are by default), Expression Design displays an arrowhead over the ending node whenever you select the object. The direction of the path affects the way certain brush strokes are displayed along the path or shape. You can reverse the direction of a path at any time.

Apply the Reverse Path Command

1. Select any shape, line, or open path in the document with the Direct Selection tool. After it is selected, Expression Design displays a colored outline around the object and an arrowhead over the ending node.

2. Apply a natural media brushstroke, such as the Dry Smooth Brush from the Acrylic category, to the selected object. Choose the preferred stroke width and color settings.

3. To reverse the direction of the path, choose **Reverse Path** from the **Object** menu, or press **Ctrl+R**. The arrowhead is repositioned and the direction of the applied brush stroke is reversed.

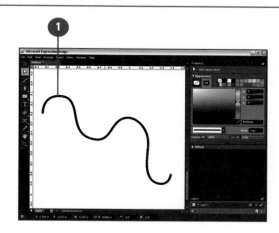

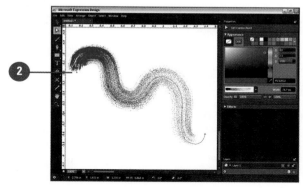

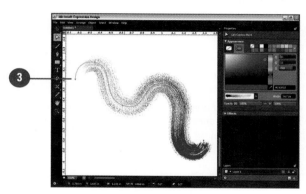

Applying Fill Color

All shapes, open and closed paths, and editable text objects can contain a fill color. You can choose a fill color using the controls available in the Appearance pane of the Properties panel. By clicking the down arrow to the right of the favorite swatches (displayed at the top of the pane), you can access the Swatch Gallery. The gallery pop-up list contains a multitude of categorized swatches that you can apply as object fills.

Enter New Fill Appearance Settings

① Select any path in the document (open or closed).

② In the **Appearance** pane of the **Properties** panel, click the **Fill** icon to bring it to the front. Choose a new fill color using any of the following methods:

◆ Using the color picker

◆ Entering RGB or hex values

◆ Clicking a saved color swatch

Expression Design displays the new fill color inside the selected object.

Did You Know?

It is possible to apply a fill color of None. To apply a fill color of None, click the Fill icon in the Appearance pane of the Properties panel and select the None color swatch.

Expression Design allows you to apply a fill color to editable text. To do so, select the text object (or multiple text objects) and follow the same steps as described previously. To change the fill color of an individual character, you must highlight it with the Text tool.

You can apply the same fill color to multiple selected paths at once. To do so, select multiple paths before applying the fill color.

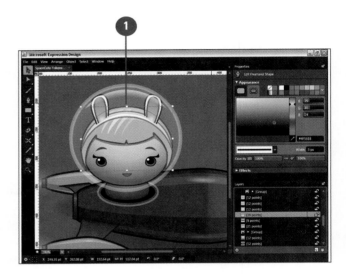

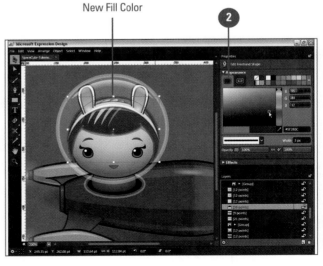

New Fill Color

Applying Image Fills

You can place an imported image inside a selected shape or path using Expression Design's Image Fill feature. This feature allows you to create dynamic design effects, such as a graphic that displays an image inside a text object or custom shape. You can access additional images from the Swatch Gallery, as descibed in the "Applying Fill Color" task.

Import an Image Fill

1. Select any path in the document (open or closed).

2. In the **Appearance** pane of the **Properties** panel, click the **Fill** icon to bring it to the front, then click the **Image Fill** swatch. Expression Design automatically applies the last used image fill inside the selected shape.

3. Click the **Import** button next to the image fill preview in the **Properties** panel.

4. In the Import Image Fill dialog box that appears, navigate to a JPEG, PNG, or TIFF image that you'd like to import and click **Open.**

   Expression Design displays the imported image inside the selected object.

> ### Did You Know?
>
> *If necessary, you can change the crop of the image by repositioning, scaling, rotating, or shearing it.* To do so, click the Transform icon to the right of the Import button to access the fly-out control panel and enter the appropriate settings.
>
> *You can also apply image fills to compound paths and editable text objects.* To do so, simply select the objects and follow the previous steps.

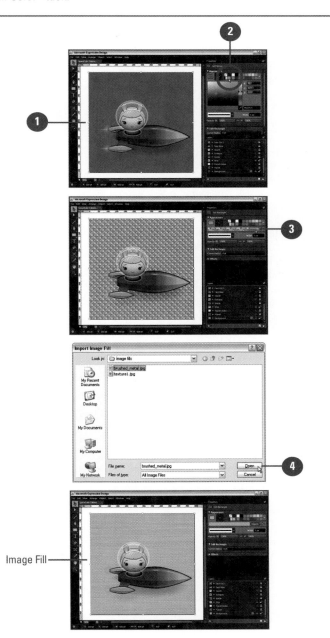

Image Fill

Transforming Image Fills

Any image that you import into an Expression Design document as an image fill can also be transformed using the Fill Transform tool or the transform controls. After it is imported, you can reposition, scale, rotate, and shear the image fill from within its path container.

Use the Fill Transform Tool

① Select any object in the document that contains an image fill.

② Access the Fill Transform tool by clicking its icon in the **Tools** panel.

> **IMPORTANT** *If the Fill Transform tool icon is not visible in the Tools panel, it is hidden behind the Gradient Transform tool. Click the Gradient Transform tool icon and hold down the mouse button to access the Fill Transform tool from the fly-out menu.*

③ To scale the image fill, click and drag a bounding box node in any direction. Hold down **Shift** as you click and drag to scale the image proportionally; hold down **Alt** as you click and drag to scale from the center of the fill.

④ To rotate the image, hover over a corner bounding box node until the cursor changes to display the Rotate icon. Click and drag to rotate the image fill.

⑤ To reposition the image fill, hover over the shape and click and drag in any direction.

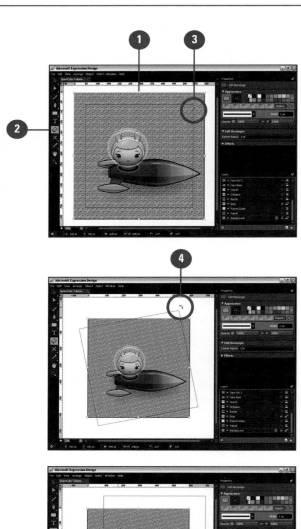

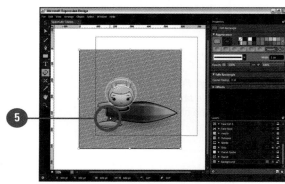

Use the Transform Controls

1. Select any object in the document that contains an image fill.

2. You can change the crop of the image by repositioning, scaling, rotating, or shearing it with the transform controls. Click the **Transform** icon to the right of the Import button to access the fly-out control panel. Enter the appropriate settings.

3. As you enter new settings in the fly-out control panel, Expression Design updates the appearance of the image fill in the document.

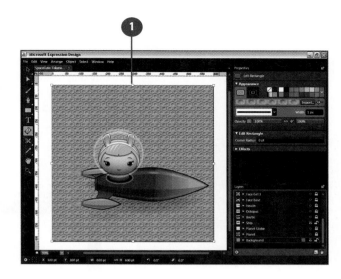

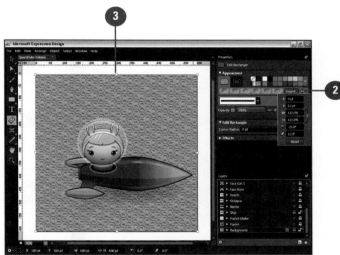

Changing Fill and Stroke Opacity

Expression Design allows you to control the opacity level for applied stroke and fill colors. By experimenting with these settings, you can create some interesting transparency effects, especially when stacking multiple transparent objects on top of each other. Note that you can also assign different opacity values to the stroke and fill of a selected object.

Lower the Opacity Value

1 Select any path, shape, or editable text object in the document that has a fill and stroke applied. Rearrange the object so that it is overlapping another object in the document.

2 With the object still selected, lower the opacity value in the fill and stroke **Opacity** fields of the **Properties** panel.

> **IMPORTANT** *If the link icon between the Opacity fields is broken, you can enter separate opacity values in each field. If it is linked, then Expression Design automatically applies the same setting to both fields.*

The selected objects are now transparent. Lowering the fill and stroke opacity allows you to see through to any objects that are placed underneath them in the document.

> **Did You Know?**
>
> *You can also lower the opacity of image fills.* To do so, select an object that contains an image fill and follow the previous steps.

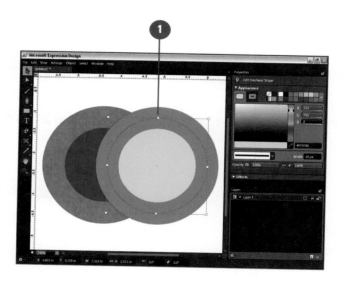

Transparent Objects

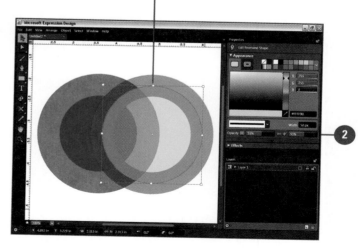

Applying Blend Modes

Change the Object Blend Mode

1 Select any path, shape, or editable text object in the document that has a fill and stroke applied. Rearrange the object so that it is overlapping another object in the document.

2 With the object selected, click the **Advanced Settings** icon (the down arrow) at the bottom of the **Appearance** pane in the **Properties** panel to access the **Blend Mode** pop-up list.

3 Select a blend mode from the pop-up list. Doing so affects both the fill and the stroke of the selected object.

The selected object is now transparent. You can see through it to any objects that are placed directly underneath it in the document. Its fill and stroke colors also blend with the colors that are applied to the objects underneath. Depending on which blend mode you choose, this can create either a darkening or lightening effect.

Did You Know?

You can also apply blend modes to objects containing image fills. To do so, select an object that contains an image fill and follow the previous steps.

You can create a different type of transparency effect by changing the applied blend mode of a selected object. By default, every object is automatically assigned the Normal blend mode setting, which has no effect. However, by choosing a different setting from the Blend Mode pop-up list, such as Multiply or Screen, the object's stroke and fill colors become transparent. As a result, the object's colors blend with any colors placed directly underneath it in the stacking order.

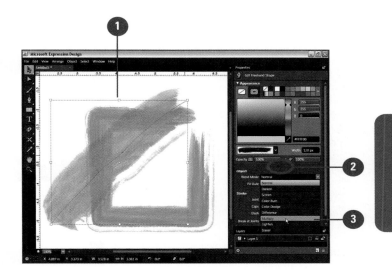

Transparent Object

Applying Gradients to Strokes and Fills

In addition to solid colors, you can also apply gradient blends as strokes and fills. Using the controls in the Appearance pane of the Properties panel, you can create a custom gradient and apply it as a stroke or fill. You can access additional preset gradients from the Swatch Gallery, as descibed previously in "Applying Fill Color." Note that none of the brush strokes in the Brush Gallery (except the Normal brush stroke) allow you to apply a gradient as a stroke color.

Create a New Gradient

1 Select any path, shape, or editable text object in the document.

2 In the **Appearance** pane of the **Properties** panel, click either the **Fill** or **Stroke** icon to bring it to the front, then click the **Gradient Color** swatch. Expression Design automatically applies the last used gradient to the fill or stroke of the selected shape.

> **TIMESAVER** *Press X to toggle between the Fill and Stroke icons in the Appearance pane.*

3 The gradient controls automatically appear underneath the color picker in the Properties panel. Click the **Linear Gradient** or **Radial Gradiant** icon to choose which type of gradient to apply.

4 Click the left color stop underneath the gradient bar to select it. Expression Design fills the tip of the color stop with black when it is selected.

5 Choose a new color for the gradient color stop using any of the following methods:

- ◆ Using the color picker

- ◆ Entering RGB or hex values

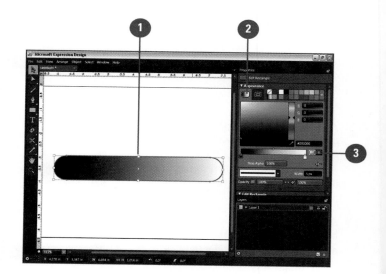

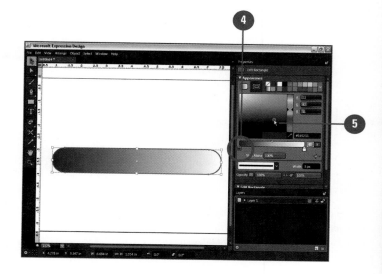

6 Now click the right color stop underneath the gradient bar and repeat step 5 to change its color.

7 If you'd like to add a third color to the gradient, click anywhere in the gradient bar to add a color stop. Continue to add as many color stops as you like to create a multi-color gradient. You can remove a color stop by simply clicking and dragging it off the gradient bar.

> **IMPORTANT** *A gradient must always contain at least two colors.*

8 Move the gradient midpoint sliders at the top of the gradient bar to set the midpoint for each gradient transition. You can also reposition each color stop to adjust the blend.

> As you create it, Expression Design displays the new gradient in the fill or stroke area of the selected object.

Did You Know?

You can also control the opacity of a gradient color stop. To do so, select a color stop and reduce its opacity by lowering the percentage in the Stop Alpha field, which is located under the gradient bar in the Properties panel.

You can save a gradient swatch. To do so, drag the Fill or Stroke icon (whichever you are working with) into the swatches list at the top of the Appearance pane.

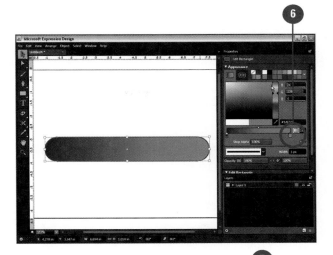

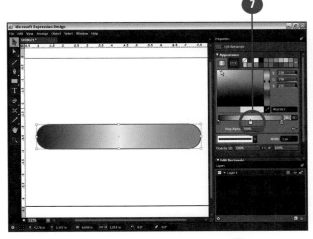

Updated Gradient

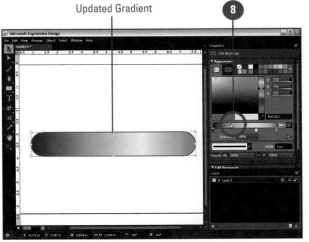

Transforming Gradients

Any gradient that you apply as a stroke or fill can also be transformed using the Gradient Transform tool or the transform controls located in the Appearance pane of the Properties panel. You can reposition, scale, and rotate a gradient at any time after it is applied to a path or editable text object.

Use the Gradient Transform Tool

① Select any object in the document that has a gradient applied to it.

② Access the Gradient Transform tool by clicking its icon in the **Tools** panel.

> **IMPORTANT** *If the Gradient Transform tool icon is not visible in the Tools panel, it is hidden behind the Fill Transform tool. Click the Fill Transform tool icon and hold down the mouse button to access the Gradient Transform tool from the fly-out menu.*

> **TIMESAVER** *Press G to access the Gradient Transform tool quickly.*

③ Click and drag in any direction that you'd like the gradient to follow. Hold down **Shift** to constrain the angle in 45 degree increments.

④ Release the mouse button to apply the new gradient angle.

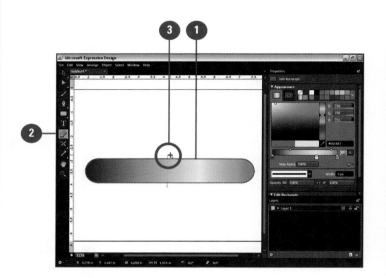

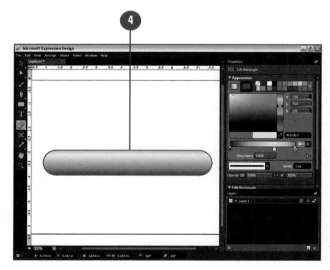

Use the Transform Controls

1. Select any object in the document that has a gradient applied to it.

2. You can transform the gradient by repositioning, scaling, or rotating it with the transofrm controls. Click the **Transform** icon to the right of the Stop Alpha field to access the fly-out control panel. Enter the appropriate settings.

   As you enter new settings in the fly-out control panel, Expression Design updates the gradient in the document.

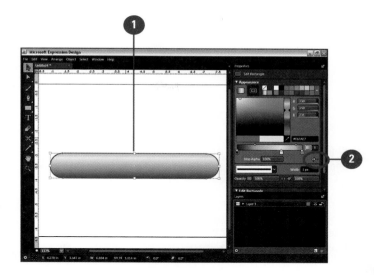

Updated Gradient

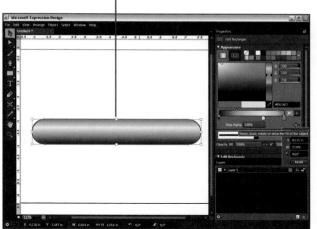

Applying Live Effects

Expression Design comes equipped with a myriad of effects that you can apply to objects. Unfortunately, this book doesn't have enough room to cover every available effect, but if you're familiar with the filters and layer styles available in Adobe Photoshop, then you already have some experience working with these types of attributes. Note that live effects are referred to as "live" because you can edit their settings at any time. This can easily be done by selecting the effect name from the Effects list and entering different settings.

Choose an Effect

1 Select any path, shape, group, imported bitmap image, or editable text object in the document.

2 In the **Effects** pane of the **Properties** panel, click the **Add Effect** icon (fx) to access the Effects fly-out list.

3 Choose an effect from one of the categories in the fly-out list. Each category has its own submenu.

4 The chosen effect appears in the Effects list in the Properties panel. Any controls associated with the effect also appear under the Effects list at the bottom of the panel. Enter the preferred settings using the various controls. Expression Design displays the results of the applied effect in the document as you adjust each setting.

5 If you'd like to add more effects to the selected object, repeat steps 3 and 4.

6 To remove a live effect from the Effects list, select it and click the **Delete Effect** button (the trash can icon).

> ### Did You Know?
>
> *You can rearrange the order of effects in the Effects list.* Expression Design allows you to change the stacking order of live effects by clicking the up or down arrows located under the Effects list.

Copying Attributes ▶

In Expression Design you have two ways to copy attributes from one object to another: using the Color Dropper or the Attribute Dropper. The Color Dropper allows you to sample a fill or stroke color from one object and apply it to the fill or stroke of another, whereas the Attribute Dropper allows you to sample both the fill and stroke color in addition to any applied effects and apply all of these attributes at once to another object.

Copy with the Color Dropper

1 Click the **Color Dropper** icon (the eyedropper) in the **Tools** panel.

> **IMPORTANT** *If the Color Dropper icon is not visible in the Tools panel, it is hidden behind the Attribute Dropper. Click the Attribute Dropper icon and hold down the mouse button to access the Color Dropper from the fly-out menu.*

> **TIMESAVER** *Press I to access the Color Dropper quickly.*

2 Hover over the fill or stroke of the object containing the color you'd like to sample. Click and hold the mouse button. The eyedropper cursor appears full.

3 Position the cursor over the fill or stroke of the object that you'd like to apply the color to.

4 Release the mouse button to apply the color.

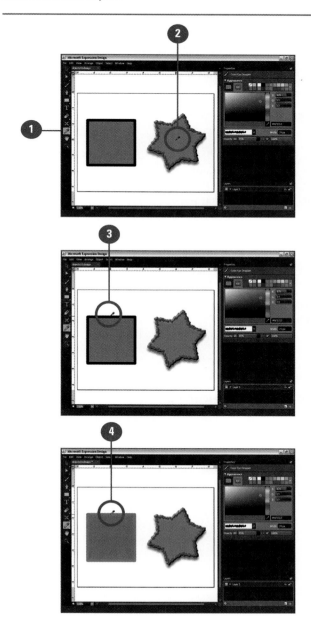

Copy with the Attribute Dropper

① Click the **Attribute Dropper** icon (the eyedropper with a star next to it) in the **Tools** panel.

IMPORTANT *If the Attribute Dropper icon is not visible in the Tools panel, it is hidden behind the Color Dropper. Click the Color Dropper icon and hold down the mouse button to access the Attribute Dropper from the fly-out menu.*

TIMESAVER *Press Shift+I to access the Attribute Dropper quickly.*

② Hover over the object containing the attributes (live effects and also fill and stroke colors) that you'd like to sample. Click and hold the mouse button.

③ Position the cursor over the object that you'd like to apply the attributes to.

④ Release the mouse button to apply the attributes.

Did You Know?

You cannot copy live effects to or from editable text objects. You can copy fill and stroke colors to and from editable text objects, but not live effects.

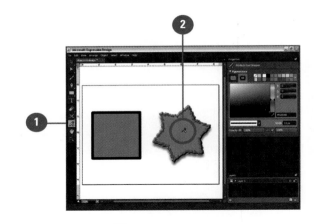

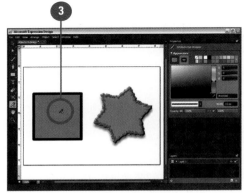

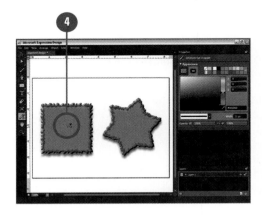

Working with
Bitmap Images

Introduction

Expression Design is, by nature, a vector-based drawing application—although it does allow you to work with and create pixel-based graphics. You can open and place bitmap graphics in this vector-based environment and, to some degree, even edit them by applying certain photographic live effects, such as those in the Adjust Colors category.

This chapter shows you the various ways that you can import bitmap graphics into your Expression Design documents, including placing them with the Import command, copying and pasting them from another application, and dragging them onto the artboard directly from Windows Explorer.

You'll learn how to use the Create Image Object feature to capture an area of a document containing vector-based artwork and save it as a bitmap graphic. In addition, you'll learn to do just the opposite by converting a bitmap graphic into vector paths using the Auto Trace feature.

Before you dig into this chapter, it's important to understand that when you import a bitmap graphic into Expression Design, it is automatically embedded into the document. A link to the source file is never established. This means that any edits applied to the original source file have no effect on the placed graphic.

What You'll Do

Open Bitmap Images

Import Bitmap Images

Copy and Paste Bitmap Images from Another Application

Import with Paste Special

Drag Bitmap Images onto the Artboard

Create Image Objects

Convert Bitmap Images to Paths

Opening Bitmap Images

Expression Design allows you to open bitmap images saved in the following file formats: TIFF, JPEG, GIF, PNG, BMP, ICO, Photoshop 7 and earlier (PSD), and Windows Media Photos (WDP, HD Photo, or HDP). When you open a bitmap image, Expression Design sizes the artboard to fit the image and places the image on Layer 1 in the document. Its current file name also appears in the Flip bar.

Apply the Open Command

① Under the **File** menu, choose **Open.**

> **TIMESAVER** *Press Ctrl+O to apply the Open command quickly.*

② In the Open File dialog box that appears, navigate to the bitmap file you'd like to open. Select the filename and click **Open.**

The document automatically appears in the work area of the interface.

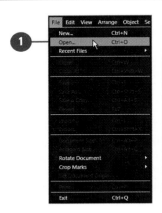

Filename

Importing Bitmap Images

Another way to work with bitmap images is to import them into an Expression Design document. When importing a bitmap image, Expression Design places it on the layer that you currently have selected in the document. Note that the Import command recognizes the same bitmap file formats as the Open command.

Apply the Import Command

1. With a document open, choose **Import** from under the **File** menu.

   TIMESAVER *Press Ctrl+I to quickly apply the Import command.*

2. In the Import Document dialog box that appears, make sure that **All Supported Formats** is chosen in the **Files of Type** field, and browse to the bitmap file on your system.

3. Click **Open** to import the bitmap image.

   Expression Design places the imported bitmap image on the layer that you currently have selected in the Layers panel.

Did You Know?

You can also import Adobe Illustrator PDFs and AI files. You can import native Illustrator files (AI), but only if the Create PDF Compatible File preference is enabled when the file is saved from Illustrator. When importing Illustrator PDFs, Expression Design does its best to convert the PDF objects into Expression Design objects, but in some cases they might be altered.

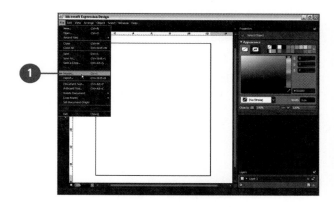

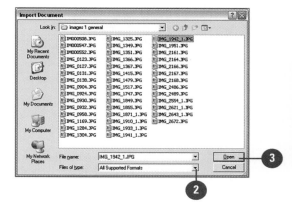

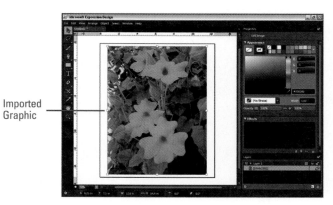

Imported Graphic

Copying and Pasting Bitmap Images from Another Application

It is also possible to select an image in another application (such as Adobe Photoshop, Adobe Fireworks, Microsoft PowerPoint, or even a web browser such as Internet Explorer or Firefox) and copy it to the Clipboard. You can then apply the Paste command in Expression Design to place it into a document.

Apply the Paste Command

1. Select a bitmap image from another application, such as Adobe Photoshop, Microsoft PowerPoint, or Internet Explorer.

2. Copy the bitmap image to the Clipboard.

3. Return to Expression Design and choose **Paste** from the **Edit** menu.

   TIMESAVER *Press Ctrl+V to apply the Paste command quickly.*

   Expression Design places the pasted bitmap image in the center of the document and at the top of the stacking order in the current layer.

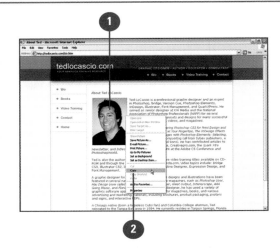

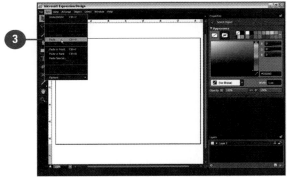

Pasted Image

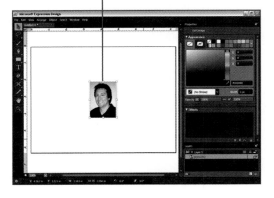

Importing with Paste Special

When pasting a bitmap graphic that you copied to the Clipboard from a separate application (such as Microsoft PowerPoint), you can use the Paste Special command to specify what file format you would like to paste the graphic as. The number of options available depends on the application that you copied the graphic from. For example, using Paste Special to paste a graphic copied from PowerPoint allows you to paste it as an Office document, PNG, GIF, or JPEG; however, pasting the same graphic copied from Photoshop does not give you any of these options.

Apply the Paste Special Command

1. Select a bitmap image from another application, such as Microsoft PowerPoint.

2. Copy the bitmap image to the Clipboard.

3. Return to Expression Design and choose **Paste Special** from the **Edit** menu.

4. In the Paste Special dialog box that appears, choose the file format that you'd like to paste the bitmap image as and click **OK**.

   Expression Design places the pasted bitmap image in the center of the document and at the top of the stacking order in the current layer.

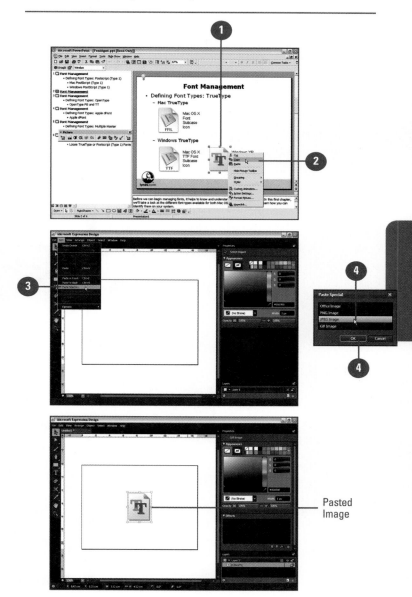

Pasted Image

Dragging Bitmap Images onto the Artboard

Expression Design also allows you to drag a bitmap image onto the artboard from Windows Explorer or from a web browser, such as Internet Explorer. Note that when you drag an image into a document, Expression Design places it on the layer that you currently have selected in the Layers panel.

Select and Drag an Image File

1. Select a bitmap image from Windows Explorer or from a web browser, such as Internet Explorer.

2. Drag the image directly onto the artboard in Expression Design.

3. Release the mouse button to place the image.

   Expression Design places the bitmap image at the top of the stacking order in the current layer.

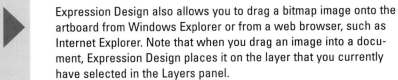

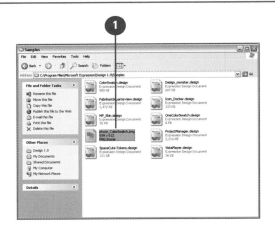

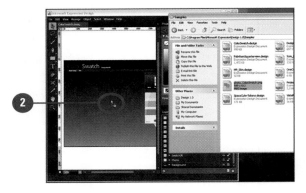

Bitmap Image

Creating Image Objects

The Create Image Object command allows you to copy a specific area of a vector graphic and convert it into a bitmap graphic (a process called "rasterization"). This process is similar to taking a screen capture of a portion of your document. The resulting image is made up entirely of pixels and cannot be edited using the vector-drawing tools, such as the Pen toolset or the Direct Selection tool.

Apply the Create Image Object Command

1 Open a document containing a vector graphic that you would like to rasterize.

2 Point to the **Object** menu, choose **Image**, and then choose **Create Image Object** from the fly-out submenu.

3 Marquee over the objects that you would like to rasterize by clicking and dragging with the Create Image Object cursor.

4 Enter a resolution setting in the **Rasterize Area** dialog box that appears and click **OK**.

The image object appears outlined at the top of the stacking order in the current layer, and in the same position as the area that you copied.

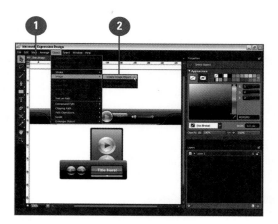

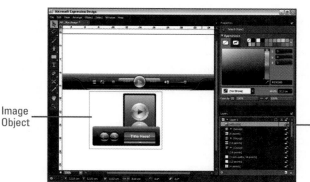

Image Object

Image Object

Converting Bitmap Images to Paths

Expression Design contains a built-in auto trace feature that allows you to convert a selected bitmap image into vector paths. The settings that you enter in the Auto Trace Image dialog box allow you to set specific Auto Trace parameters, including the number of colors to use and the amount of image details to preserve.

Apply the Auto Trace Image Command

1 Select any image object in the document.

2 Point to the **Object** menu, choose **Image**, and then choose **Auto Trace Image** from the fly-out submenu.

3 Set the Auto Trace parameters in the Auto Trace Image dialog box that appears:

◆ **Number of Colors**—Enter a value to specify the number of colors that Expression Design should use for the traced vector image.

◆ **Pre-filtering**—Enter a value to indicate the amount of smoothing that should be applied to the bitmap image before converting it to vector paths. The higher the value, the more it will be smoothed.

◆ **Tightness of Fit**—Choose a tightness setting from the drop-down list to specify how tight you would like the vector paths to fit the original bitmap image. Higher settings preserve more image detail and result in more path nodes.

4 Click **OK** to apply the Auto Trace settings.

5 Expression Design converts the image to vector paths. Click in a blank area of the document to deselect the paths and view the converted image.

Working with Text Objects

Introduction

Not every design created in Expression Design is made up solely of paths, shapes, and bitmap graphics. In fact, a good number of them also include text. No matter if it's a few simple words or a full story containing many paragraphs, Expression Design makes creating and formatting text simple.

In this chapter, you'll learn how to use the Text tool to insert text into your documents. You'll also learn how to format selected text using the various settings in the Text pane of the Properties panel.

This chapter also shows you how to insert text along a path or inside a shape (also referred to as area text). This includes combining preexisting text objects with shapes and paths via the Attach Text or Attach Area Text commands.

The last section describes how to convert your text objects into vector paths that can be edited with the various drawing tools, such as the Pen toolset, Scissors, and Direct Selection tool.

Creating Text

To work with text, you must first add some to your documents. In Expression Design, this can be done by typing with the Text tool. Although it is possible to copy text from a separate application, such as Microsoft Word or Excel, and paste it with the Text tool, it is not possible to use the Import command to import text from a Word DOC, TXT, or RTF file.

Type with the Text Tool

1 Access the Text tool by clicking its icon (the letter T) in the **Tools** panel.

> **TIMESAVER** *Press T to access the Text tool quickly.*

2 Click once anywhere on the artboard to insert the Text tool cursor. You'll know it's inserted when you see it flashing.

3 Enter the text into your document by typing. The characters automatically take on the default text attributes that are set in the Text pane of the Properties panel. They also take on the fill and stroke attributes currently set in the Appearance pane.

Did You Know?

You can also apply fills and strokes to editable text. To do so, select the text object (or multiple text objects) and follow the steps described in Chapter 9, "Applying Fills, Strokes, and Effects." To apply fills and strokes to individual characters, you must highlight them with the Text tool.

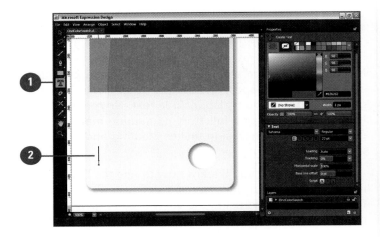

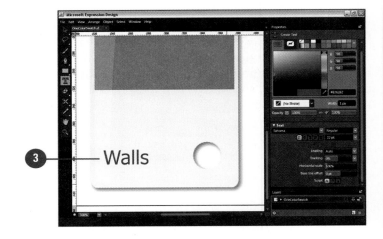

Formatting Text Objects

Text objects contain their own set of formatting attributes that you can access from the Text pane of the Properties panel. These attributes are divided into two sections of the Text pane: basic and advanced. Basic attributes include font, font decoration (or style), point size, and horizontal alignment. Advanced attributes include leading, tracking, horizontal scale, baseline offset, and script setting.

Enter Basic Text Properties

1 Select an editable text object with the Selection tool.

> **IMPORTANT** *To change the attributes for individual characters within a text object, you must click and drag over them with the Text tool.*

2 In the **Text** pane of the **Properties** panel, enter a different point size in the **Type Size** field or choose a size from the drop-down list.

3 Choose a different font from the **Font Family** drop-down list (also called the **Font Gallery**). If the font you choose contains more than one style, such as Bold or Italic, you can choose it from the **Font Decoration** drop-down list.

4 Choose a horizontal alignment option by clicking one of the text align buttons located under the Font Family field. These settings have more of an effect when you apply them to multiple lines of text rather than a single line. Options include Align Left, Align Center, Align Right, Justify, and Justify All.

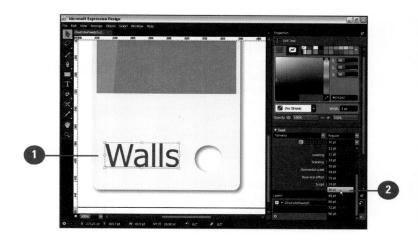

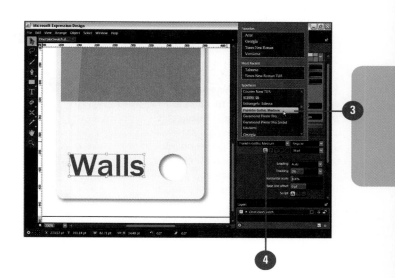

Enter Advanced Text Properties

1. Select an editable text object with the Selection tool.

   IMPORTANT *To change the attributes for individual characters within a text object, you must click and drag over them with the Text tool to select them.*

2. To specify the amount of vertical space to place between lines of a selected paragraph, enter a percentage into the Leading field or choose a setting from the drop-down list. By default Expression Design places an automatic amount of space between lines for you, which is the Auto setting. The leading percentage you choose is actually a percentage of the chosen font size.

3. To specify the amount of horizontal space to place between individual characters, enter a percentage into the **Tracking** field or choose a value from the drop-down list. Positive values add space; negative values remove space.

Did You Know?

You can also adjust the amount of space placed between two characters (referred to as "kerning.") To adjust the amount of horizontal space that is placed between two adjacent characters, select the first character of the pair with the Text tool and apply a Tracking value to it in the Text pane of the Properties panel.

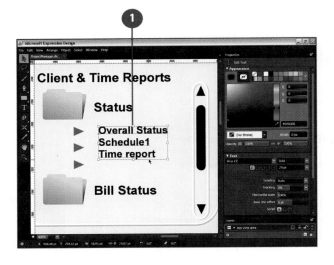

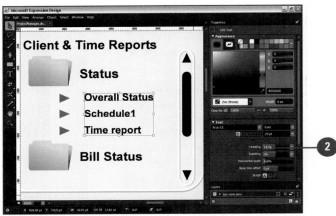

4 To change the width of the text, enter a percentage into the **Horizontal Scale** field.

5 To change the baseline shift and size of selected characters, click the **Superscript** or **Subscript** buttons. Superscript places the reduced text above the baseline; Subscript places it below.

6 To move selected characters above or below the baseline, enter the number of points into the **Baseline Offset** field. Positive values place the characters above the baseline; negative values place the characters below the baseline.

Did You Know?

The Font Gallery also contains a Favorites and Most Recent list. Just like the Brush Gallery and Swatches Gallery, the Font Gallery also contains a Favorites list and a Most Recent list. You can add to the Favorites by dragging a selected font from the Typeface list into the Favorites list. The Most Recent list displays the last two typefaces that you used.

Adding Text to Paths

You can insert text along a path so that it flows along every corner and curve, or you can apply Expression Design's Area Text feature, which allows you to insert text to fill a shape. One way that you can do this is by typing with the Text tool; another way is by using the Attach Text or Attach Area Text commands, which allow you to combine preexisting text objects with selected paths or shapes.

Type Text on a Path

① Click the **Text** tool icon in the **Tools** panel, or press **T**.

② Hover over a path with the Text tool until the cursor changes to display a curved line. Click anywhere along the path to insert the Text tool cursor. This is now the starting position for the text.

③ Enter the text by typing. The characters automatically take on the text attributes that are set in the Text pane of the Properties panel. They also take on the fill and stroke attributes that are currently set in the Appearance pane.

④ To reposition the starting point for the text, place the cursor over the left edge of the first character until the cursor changes to display two arrows. Click and drag in either direction to reposition the text along the path.

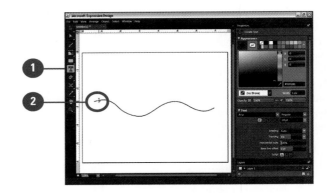

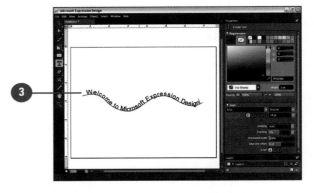

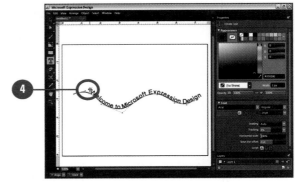

Did You Know?

A path retains its appearance attributes after you add text to it. Any stroke or fill attributes that you've applied to a path remain intact after you add text to it.

Attach Text to a Path

① Select any shape, line, or open path in the document.

② Shift+click or marquee over any text object in the document to add it to your selection.

③ Under the **Object** menu, point to **Text on Path** and choose **Attach Text** from the fly-out submenu.

Expression Design places the text along the path.

④ When attaching text to a path, Expression Design always uses the starting point for the path as the starting point for the text. To reposition the starting point for the text, place the cursor over the left edge of the first character until the cursor changes to display two arrows. Click and drag in either direction to reposition the text along the path.

Did You Know?

You can select text along a path and edit its appearance attributes at any time. It is possible to select text along a path and change its stroke and fill attributes or any of the settings located in the Text pane of the Properties panel.

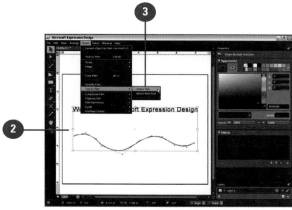

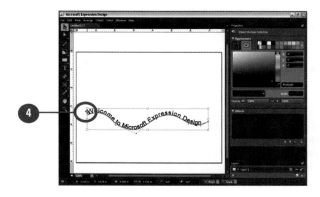

Insert Area Text

1. Click the **Text** tool icon in the **Tools** panel, or press **T**.

2. Hold down **Shift** and hover over a closed path with the Text tool until the cursor changes to display a closed path around it.

3. Shift+click anywhere along the path to insert the Text tool cursor. Expression Design automatically selects the path and outlines it with the current layer color.

   IMPORTANT *If the object contains a fill color, you can also Shift+click anywhere inside the shape; however, if no fill color is applied, you must Shift+click along the edge of the path.*

4. Enter the area text by typing. The characters automatically take on the default text attributes that are set in the Text pane of the Properties panel.

   As you type, Expression Design automatically wraps the lines of text to fit inside the shape. However, if the last line is too long, Expression Design allows it to extend outside the shape rather than clipping it off and marking it as overset.

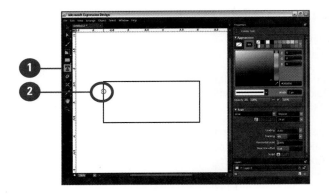

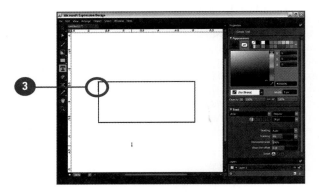

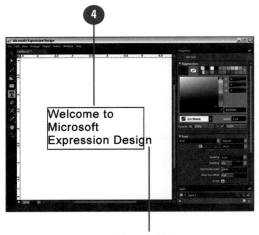

Extended Type

Attach Area Text

① Select any closed path in the document with the Selection tool.

② Shift+click or marquee over any text object in the document to add it to your selection.

③ Under the **Object** menu, point to **Text on Path** and choose **Attach Area Text** from the fly-out submenu.

Expression Design places the text inside the path and automatically wraps the lines of text to fit inside. However, if the last line is too long, Expression Design allows it to extend outside the shape rather than clipping it off and marking it as overset.

Did You Know?

Double-clicking a text object with any of the selection tools automatically causes you to switch to the Text tool. You can access the Text tool quickly by double-clicking a text object with any of the selection-making tools (Selection, Direct Selection, Lasso Selection, and Group Select). Expression Design inserts the Text tool cursor at the exact point where you double-clicked.

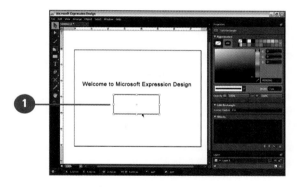

Area Text

Release Text

1. Select any text path object (text along a path or area text) in the document.

2. Under the **Object** menu, point to **Text on Path** and choose **Release Text** from the fly-out submenu.

   Expression Design releases the text from the path and retains any appearance attributes that were applied to both.

Released Text

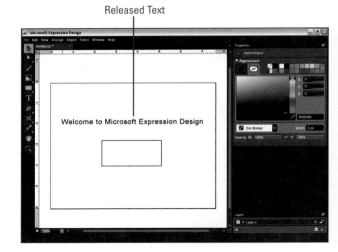

Converting Text to Paths

Expression Design also allows you to convert selected text objects to vector paths. Generally, this is something you should only do if you'd like to alter the shape of the individual characters with the vector-drawing tools. This is because converting text to paths means forfeiting the ability to edit the text with the Text tool. After the text object is converted, you can no longer use the Text tool to enter or remove text, or apply different formatting attributes in the Text pane of the Properties panel.

Apply the Convert Object to Path Command

① Select any editable text object in the document.

② Under the **Object** menu, choose **Convert Object to Path**.

> **TIMESAVER** *Press Ctrl+Shift+O to apply the Convert Object to Path command quickly.*

The text object is converted to vector paths and its characters are automatically grouped together. Characters containing transparent areas, such as O and P, are converted into compound paths.

You can no longer edit the text with the Text tool; however, you can use the vector-drawing tools, such as the Pen toolset, the Scissors, or the Direct Selection tool to edit the paths that make up each character.

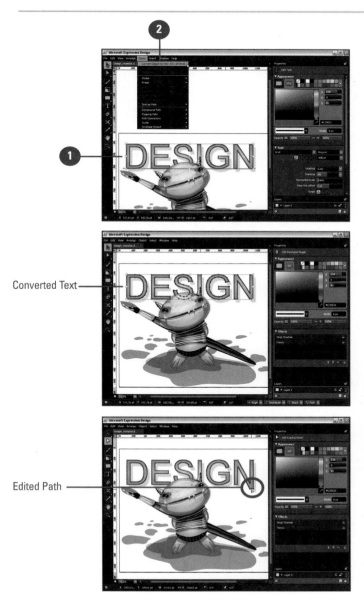

Converted Text —

Edited Path —

Transforming Objects

Introduction

When referring to a creative graphics application like Expression Design, the term "transforming objects" means moving, scaling, rotating, skewing, flipping, or warping selected objects in the document.

You've already learned how to move objects by following the lessons described in Chapter 6, "Working with Objects." This chapter takes it a bit further by showing you the different ways that you can scale, rotate, and skew objects. This includes transforming objects with the Selection tool and using the controls available in the Action bar.

This chapter also shows you how to transform objects using the various rotate and reflect commands. The rotate commands allow you to rotate a selected object 90° clockwise or counterclockwise or rotate 180°. The reflect commands allow you to flip an object horizontally or vertically.

In addition, this chapter explains how to repeat, reset, and commit transformations by applying the various commands located under the Transform submenu. The last two sections describe how you can warp paths, shapes, text objects, and placed bitmap graphics by repositioning selected points in the warp grid and how you can create new shapes by applying the Path Operations commands to overlapping paths.

Scaling Objects

Aside from moving an object (as described in Chapter 6, "Working with Objects"), one of the most commonly applied transformations is the ability to resize or "scale" an object. In Expression Design, there are two different ways that you can scale a selected path, shape, text object, or placed bitmap graphic: by clicking and dragging a bounding box node with the Selection tool or by entering new values in the Width and Height fields of the Action bar.

Scale an Object Using the Selection Bounding Box Nodes

1. Access the Selection tool by clicking its icon (the black arrow) in the **Tools** panel.

   TIMESAVER *Press V to access the Selection tool quickly.*

2. Click or marquee over any object(s) in the document to make a selection with the Selection tool. You know you have a selection when the blue bounding box appears around the object(s).

3. Hover over any of the bounding box nodes with the Selection tool. As you do, the cursor changes to display a double-sided arrow.

4. Click and drag a bounding box node in any direction to scale the object.

   IMPORTANT *To scale an object proportionally, hold down Shift as you click and drag one of the bounding box nodes.*

Did You Know?

Enabling the Scale Stroke Width option allows you to increase or decrease an object's stroke width as you scale it. To access the Scale Stroke Width option from the Options dialog box, point to Options under the Edit menu and choose Stroke from the fly-out submenu.

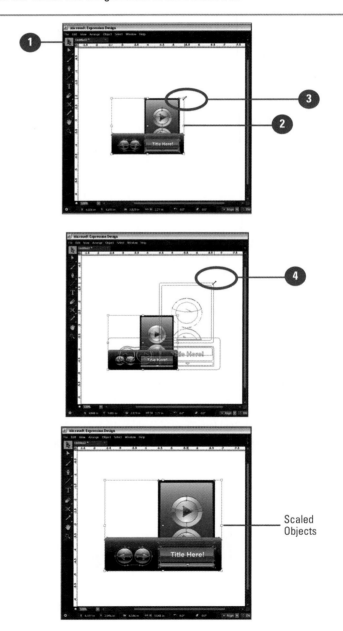

Scaled Objects

Scale an Object Using the Action Bar

1 Click the **Selection** tool icon in the **Tools** panel, or press **V**.

2 Click or marquee over any object(s) in the document to make a selection with the Selection tool. You know you have a selection when the blue bounding box appears around the object(s).

3 The Action bar displays the exact width and height measurements for the currently selected object. Enter new values into the **W** and **H** fields to scale the object.

IMPORTANT *If the link icon between the W and H fields is closed, you can enter a value in either field and Expression Design will scale the object proportionally.*

Did You Know?

By default, Expression Design transforms all objects from the center. When rotating, scaling, or skewing an object with the Selection tool or the Action bar controls, Expression Design uses the object's center as its pivot point. You can change the pivot point by clicking any of the white squares in the Registration Point icon located on the far left of the Action bar.

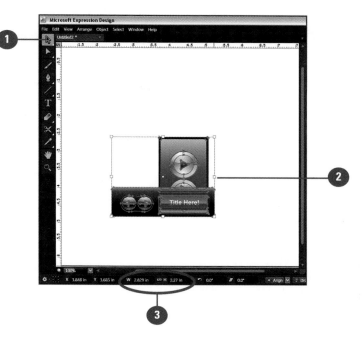

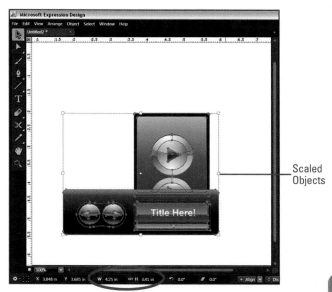

Scaled Objects

Rotating Objects

Rotating objects is another commonly used transformation technique. As it is with scaling, you can rotate a selected path, shape, text object, or placed bitmap graphic using the Selection tool or by entering a value into the Rotation Angle field in the Action bar. You can also apply any of the rotate commands, including Rotate 90° Clockwise, Rotate 90° Counterclockwise, and Rotate 180°.

Rotate an Object Using the Selection Bounding Box Nodes

1. Click the **Selection** tool icon in the **Tools** panel, or press **V**.

2. Click or marquee over any object(s) in the document to make a selection with the Selection tool. You know you have a selection when the blue bounding box appears around the object(s).

3. Hover the cursor next to (not directly over) any corner bounding box node. As you do, the cursor changes to display a rounded arrow.

4. Click and drag in either direction to rotate the object.

   IMPORTANT *To constrain your rotation to the number of Rotation Steps specified in the Units and Grids pane of the Options dialog box, hold down Shift as you click and drag.*

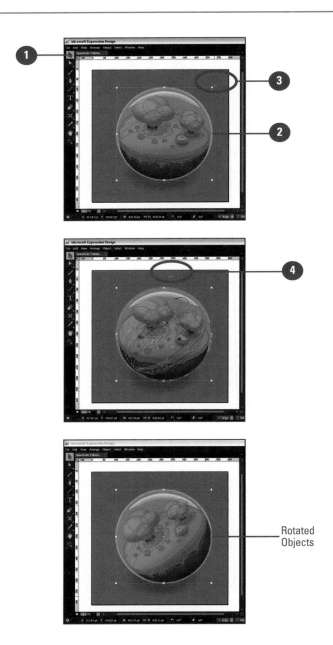

Rotated Objects

Rotate an Object Using the Action Bar

1. Click the **Selection** tool icon in the **Tools** panel, or press **V**.

2. Click or marquee over any object(s) in the document to make a selection with the Selection tool. You know you have a selection when the blue bounding box appears around the object(s).

3. Enter a new value into the **Rotation Angle** field of the Action bar. Negative values rotate the object(s) clockwise; positive values rotate counterclockwise.

Did You Know?

Expression Design allows you to transform an object's image fill along with the object itself. When the Transform Image Fill option is enabled, Expression Design applies all object transformations (moving, rotating, scaling, and skewing) to an object's image fill and the object itself. When this option is disabled, all object transformations are applied to the object, but not to the image fill. To access the Transform Image Fill option from the Options dialog box, point to Options under the Edit menu and choose General from the fly-out submenu.

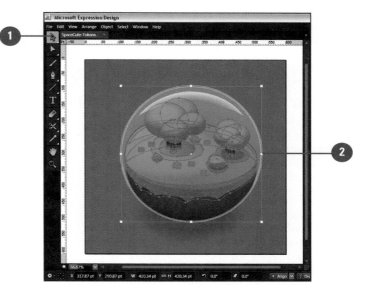

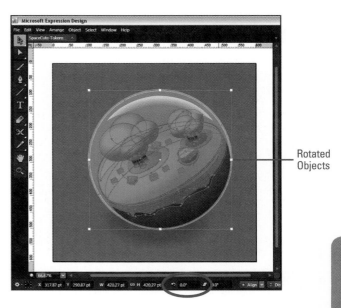

Rotated Objects

Rotate an Object Using the Rotate Commands

1. Click the **Selection** tool icon in the **Tools** panel, or press **V**.

2. Click or marquee over any object(s) in the document to make a selection with the Selection tool. You know you have a selection when the blue bounding box appears around the object(s).

3. Under the **Arrange** menu, point to **Transform** and choose **Rotate 90° Clockwise, Rotate 90° Counterclockwise,** or **Rotate 180°** from the fly-out submenu.

   Expression Design applies the transformation to the selected object.

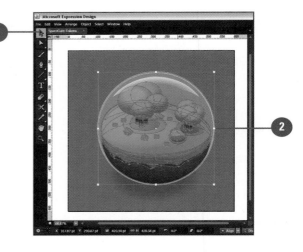

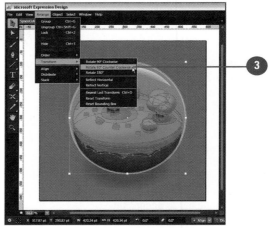

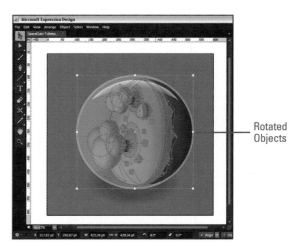

Rotated Objects

Skewing Objects

Expression Design also allows you to skew objects. You can skew any selected path, shape, text object, or placed bitmap graphic by clicking and dragging any side bounding box node with the Selection tool or by entering a value into the Skew Angle field of the Action bar.

Skew an Object Using the Selection Bounding Box Nodes

① Click the **Selection** tool icon in the **Tools** panel, or press **V**.

② Click or marquee over any object(s) in the document to make a selection with the Selection tool. You know you have a selection when the blue bounding box appears around the object(s).

③ Hover the cursor next to (not directly over) any side bounding box node. As you do, the cursor changes to display the angled skew cursor.

④ To skew the object, click and drag in either direction (left or right for top and bottom nodes; up or down for left or right nodes).

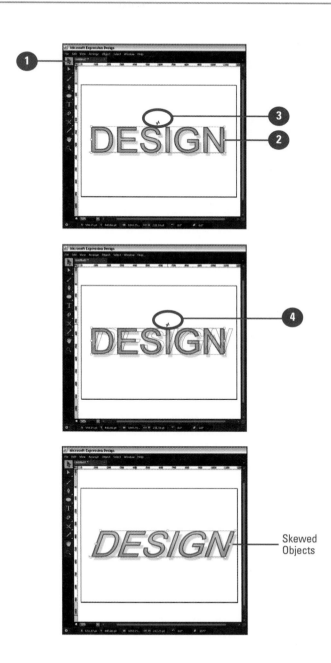

Skewed Objects

Skew an Object Using the Action Bar

1. Click the **Selection** tool icon in the **Tools** panel, or press **V**.

2. Click or marquee over any object(s) in the document to make a selection with the Selection tool. You know you have a selection when the blue bounding box appears around the object(s).

3. Enter a new value into the **Skew Angle** field of the Action bar. Negative values skew the object(s) to the left; positive values skew to the right.

Did You Know?

You can also apply object transformations to grouped objects. Expression Design allows you to move, scale, rotate, or skew grouped objects using any of the controls in the Action Bar. You can also transform grouped objects with the Selection tool using any of the methods described in this chapter.

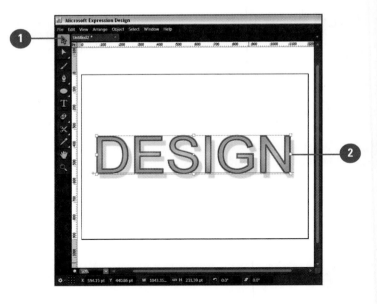

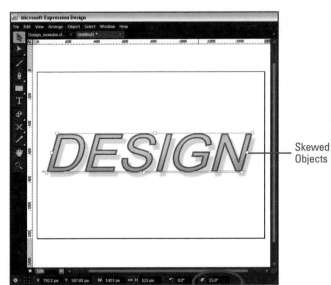

Skewed Objects

Flipping Objects

Another type of transformation that Expression Design offers you is the ability to flip objects. By applying the Reflect Horizontal or Reflect Vertical commands, you can flip a selected path, shape, text object, or placed bitmap graphic to face the opposite direction.

Apply the Reflect Commands

① Select any path, shape, text object, or placed bitmap in the document with the Selection tool.

② Under the **Arrange** menu, point to **Transform** and choose **Reflect Horizontal** or **Reflect Vertical** from the fly-out submenu.

Expression Design flips the selected object horizontally or vertically.

Did You Know?

You can also access the Transform commands from the contextual menu. Select the object you'd like to transform and right-click to access the Transform commands from the contextual menu.

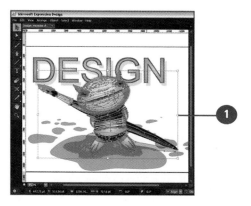

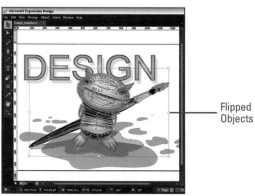

Flipped Objects

Repeating Transformations

Expression Design allows you to apply the last used transformation settings to whatever object you have selected in the document. This feature can be used to ensure that multiple objects are rotated, skewed, scaled, or even moved in exactly the same way.

Apply the Repeat Last Transform Command

1. Select any object in the document (path, shape, text object, or placed bitmap) with the Selection tool.

2. Use any of the techniques described in this chapter to apply a transformation (move, scale, rotate, flip, or skew) to the selected object.

3. Under the **Arrange** menu, point to **Transform** and choose **Repeat Last Transform** from the fly-out submenu.

   TIMESAVER *Press Ctrl+D to apply the Repeat Last Transform command quickly.*

   Expression Design applies the same transformation to the selected object.

Did You Know?

You can also apply the Repeat Last Transform command to other objects. Expression Design allows you to select a different object and apply the same transformation.

Transformed Object

Resetting Transformations

One of the unique features of Expression Design is that you can revert a selected object back to its original state, before any transformations were applied. Expression Design remembers how the object originally appeared even after you close the document.

Apply the Reset Transform Command

1 Use the Selection tool to select any path or shape that has been transformed (moved, scaled, rotated, flipped, or skewed).

2 Under the **Arrange** menu, point to **Transform** and choose **Reset Transform** from the fly-out submenu.

Expression Design reverts the selected object to its original state before any transformations were applied.

Did You Know?

The Reset Transform command has no effect on text objects. Expression Design does not allow you to reset transformations made to text objects.

Image fills that have been transformed with the Fill Transform tool can also be reset. Expression Design does allow you to reset transformations made to image fills with the Fill Transform tool.

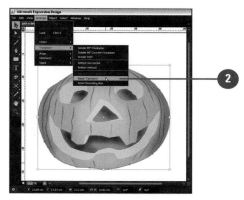

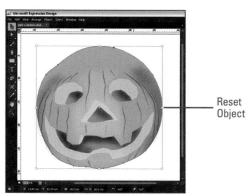

Reset Object

Committing Transformations

By applying the Reset Bounding Box command, you can replace the original state of the image (before any transformations were applied) with its current state (after transformations have been applied). From then on, Expression Design refers to this state whenever you apply the Reset Transform command.

Apply the Reset Bounding Box Command

① Use the Selection tool to select any object in the document that has been transformed (moved, scaled, rotated, flipped, or skewed).

② Under the **Arrange** menu, point to **Transform** and choose **Reset Bounding Box** from the fly-out submenu.

③ Expression Design commits all transformations that have been applied to the selected object. As a result, the Reset Transform and Reset Bounding Box commands are no longer accessible from the Transform submenu.

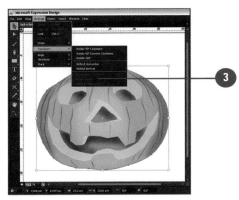

Warping Objects

Warping is a technique that allows you to squeeze and stretch different areas of an object. You can distort selected shapes, paths, text objects, and placed bitmap graphics by repositioning points along the overlying warp grid with the Direct Selection tool. Expression Design also allows you to control the amount of points contained within the grid.

Apply the Make Warp Group Command

1 Select any path, shape, or text object in the document. You can also select multiple objects or grouped objects.

> **IMPORTANT** *You do not need to create a warp group to warp a placed bitmap graphic.*

2 Under the **Object** menu, point to **Envelope Distort** and choose **Make Warp Group** from the fly-out submenu.

> **TIMESAVER** *Press Ctrl+Alt+W to apply the Make Warp Group command quickly.*

3 Expression Design displays a grid over the object (also referred to as a mesh). You can select individual points in the grid by clicking them with the Direct Selection tool. Shift+click or marquee to select multiple points.

Reposition the grid points with the Direct Selection tool (or Lasso Selection tool) to warp the object.

Did You Know?

You can reset the warp grid at any time. Expression Design allows you to revert the warp grid back to its original state before any points were moved. To do so, select the warp group object. Then under the Object menu, point to Envelope Distort and choose Reset Grid.

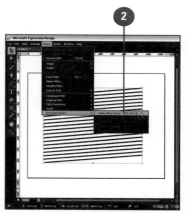

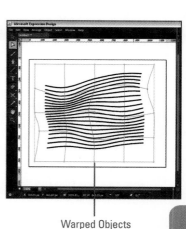

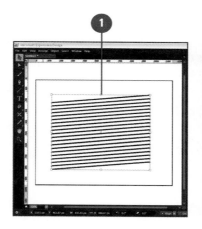

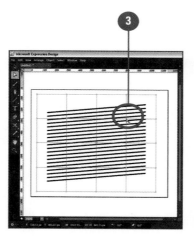

Warped Objects

Increase or Decrease Resolution

1. Select any warp group object in the document.

2. Under the **Object** menu, point to **Envelope Distort** and choose **Increase Resolution** or **Decrease Resolution** from the fly-out submenu.

   TIMESAVER *Press Ctrl+. (period) to apply the Increase Resolution command; press Ctrl+, (comma) to apply the Decrease Resolution command.*

   The Increase Resolution command adds points to the warp grid; Decrease Resolution removes points.

Did You Know?

To reveal the warp grid for a placed bitmap graphic, you must apply the Increase Resolution command. It is not necessary to apply the Make Warp Group command for a placed bitmap graphic. Simply apply the Increase Resolution command and the overlying mesh will appear.

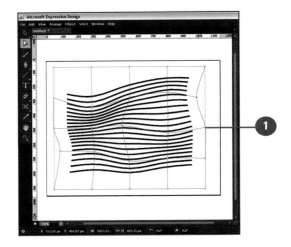

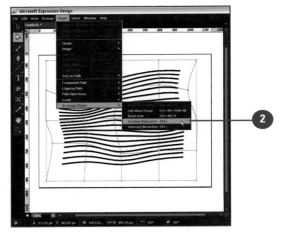

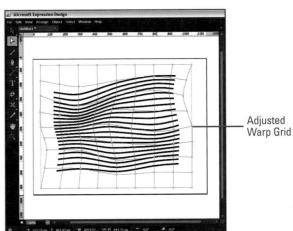

Adjusted Warp Grid

Edit the Warp Group Object

1 Select any warp group object in the document.

2 Under the **Object** menu, point to **Envelope Distort** and choose **Edit Warp Group** from the fly-out submenu.

TIMESAVER *Press Ctrl+Alt+Shift+W to apply the Edit Warp Group command quickly.*

3 Expression Design displays the unwarped object in a separate document window. Edit the object using any of the path editing tools, such as the Pen toolset, Scissors, and Direct Selection tool. You can also edit any of its applied attributes such as fill, stroke, or live effect settings.

4 Choose **Close** from the **File** menu, or click the window's close button in the Flip bar.

Expression Design updates the warp group object in the document.

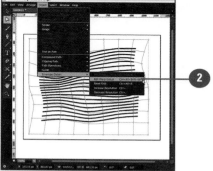

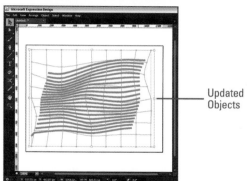

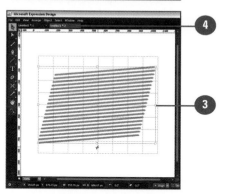

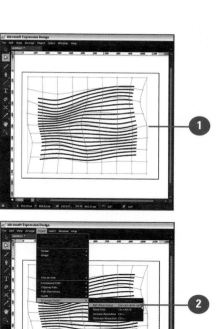

Updated Objects

Ungroup Warp Transformations

1. Select any warp group object in the document.

2. Choose **Ungroup** from the **Arrange** menu.

   TIMESAVER *Press Ctrl+Shift+G to apply the Ungroup command quickly.*

   Expression Design removes the grid from the object but retains the warp effect. All shape edits made with the warp grid are converted into Bézier points.

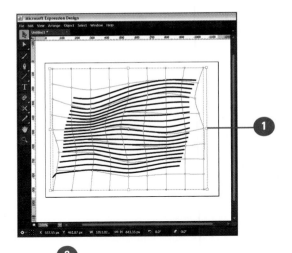

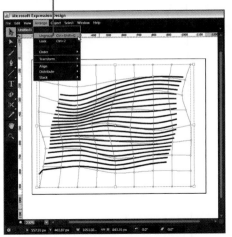

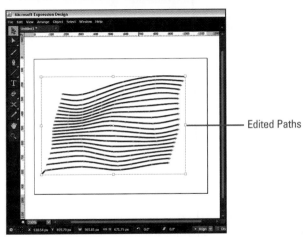

Edited Paths

Applying Path Operations

The Path Operations commands allow you to control how overlapping paths interact with each other to create new shapes. Options include Unite, Front Minus Back, Back Minus Front, Intersect, and Divide. Note that applying these commands to selected shapes and paths actually changes their path structure.

Apply the Unite Command

① Use the shape tools (Rectangle, Ellipse, or Polygon) to create two shapes that overlap each other. If you prefer, you could also draw two custom shapes using the Pen tool.

② Apply a different fill color to each shape using any of the techniques described in Chapter 9, "Applying Fills, Strokes, and Effects."

③ Select both objects by Shift+clicking or drawing a marquee with the Selection tool.

④ Under the **Object** menu, point to **Path Operations** and choose **Unite** from the fly-out submenu.

Expression Design combines the shapes into a single path.

Did You Know?

Paths combined with Path Operations always inherit the attributes of the top object in the stacking order. When combining shapes with the Path Operations commands, Expression Design always applies the attributes from the top object in the stacking order to the new shape. Any attributes already applied to the underlying object are lost.

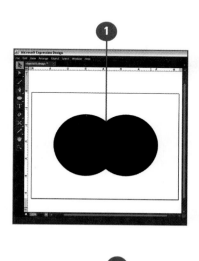

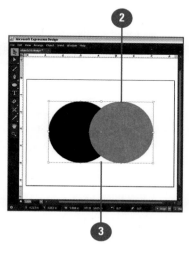

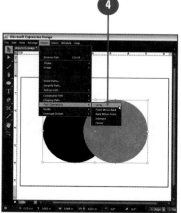

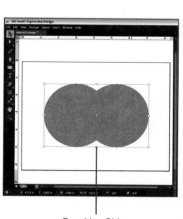

Resulting Object

Apply the Front Minus Back Command

1. Use the shape tools (Rectangle, Ellipse, or Polygon) to create two shapes that overlap each other. If you prefer, you could also draw two custom shapes using the Pen tool.

2. Apply a different fill color to each shape using any of the techniques described in Chapter 9, "Applying Fills, Strokes, and Effects."

3. Select both objects by Shift+clicking or drawing a marquee with the Selection tool.

4. Under the **Object** menu, point to **Path Operations** and choose **Front Minus Back** from the fly-out submenu.

Expression Design removes the underlying shape and alters the path of the top shape by cutting out the area where the two overlapped.

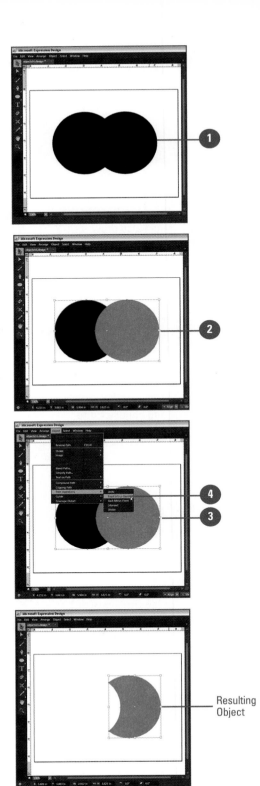

Resulting Object

Apply the Back Minus Front Command

1. Use the shape tools (Rectangle, Ellipse, or Polygon) to create two shapes that overlap each other. If you prefer, you could also draw two custom shapes using the Pen tool.

2. Apply a different fill color to each shape using any of the techniques described in Chapter 9, "Applying Fills, Strokes, and Effects."

3. Select both objects by Shift+clicking or drawing a marquee with the Selection tool.

4. Under the **Object** menu, point to **Path Operations** and choose **Back Minus Front** from the fly-out submenu.

   Expression Design removes the top shape and alters the path of the underlying shape by cutting out the area where the two overlapped.

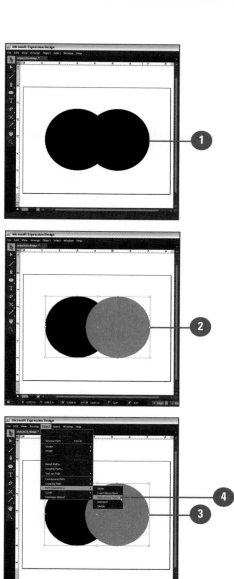

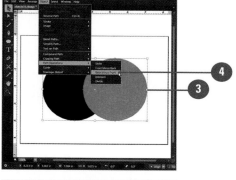

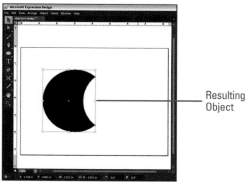

Resulting Object

Apply the Intersect Command

1 Use the shape tools (Rectangle, Ellipse, or Polygon) to create two shapes that overlap each other. If you prefer, you could also draw two custom shapes using the Pen tool.

2 Apply a different fill color to each shape using any of the techniques described in Chapter 9, "Applying Fills, Strokes, and Effects."

3 Select both objects by Shift+clicking or drawing a marquee with the Selection tool.

4 Under the **Object** menu, point to **Path Operations** and choose **Intersect** from the fly-out submenu.

Expression Design creates a single path based on the area where the two shapes intersect. All other areas are deleted.

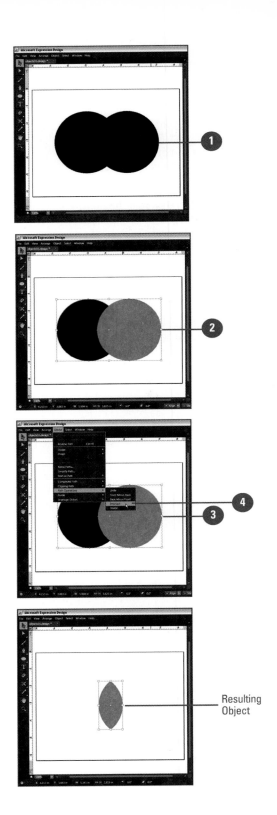

Resulting Object

Apply the Divide Command

1 Use the shape tools (Rectangle, Ellipse, or Polygon) to create two shapes that overlap each other. If you prefer, you could also draw two custom shapes using the Pen tool.

2 Apply a different fill color to each shape using any of the techniques described in Chapter 9, "Applying Fills, Strokes, and Effects."

3 Select both objects by Shift+clicking or drawing a marquee with the Selection tool.

4 Under the **Object** menu, point to **Path Operations** and choose **Divide** from the fly-out submenu.

Expression Design divides the two shapes into multiple paths.

See Also

See Chapter 8, "Drawing Shapes and Paths" to learn more about paths and path structure in Expression Design.

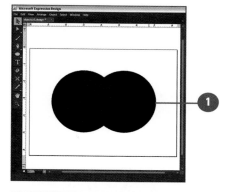

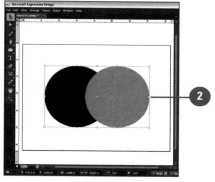

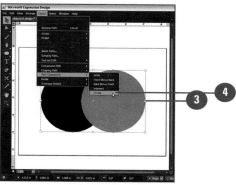

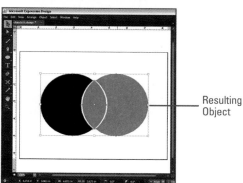

Resulting Object

Exporting and Printing

13

Introduction

Now that you know everything there is to know about creating graphics in Expression Design, it's time to learn how to output them. What does "output" mean, you might ask? Well, when working with a graphics application like Expression Design, the term output refers to the process of exporting or printing a document.

In this final chapter, you'll learn how to define the area of your artwork that you'd like to print or export by adding crop marks to the document. You'll also learn how to apply the Pixel Preview option, which allows you to simulate onscreen what your artwork will look like when exporting to a specific bitmap file format, such as JPEG, GIF, PNG, or TIFF.

This chapter also walks you through the process of setting up your Print and Export options and understanding the settings in the Print Rasterization Settings dialog box.

The remaining tasks in this chapter explain how to export your graphics in every file format that is available under the Save As File Type list. Special emphasis is placed on how to export your graphics into the native Expression XAML language format. By exporting XAML, you can open and edit your Expression Design graphics in other XAML applications, such as Expression Blend. You can also export XAML graphics that are compatible with applications supporting Microsoft Silverlight—a cross-platform browser plug-in that is used to display video, animations, and interactive applications over the web.

Defining Crop Marks

By adding crop marks to a document, you can define the image areas that you would like to print or export. The crop marks are visual guides only and are not considered part of the artwork. As a result, the crop marks do not appear on the printed page or in the exported file. Expression Design allows you to set crop marks in three different ways: manually, by entering coordinates in the Set Crop Marks dialog box, or by basing them on a selection.

Set Crop Marks Manually

1 With a document open, select **Crop Marks** from the **File** menu, and choose **Set** from the fly-out submenu.

> **TIMESAVER** *Press Ctrl+Alt+Shift+C to apply the Set command quickly.*

2 Click and drag a rectangular marquee over the portion of the document that you'd like to print or export. Use the cursor guides to help define the area.

When you release the mouse button, Expression Design adds a crop mark in each corner of the defined area.

Did You Know?

You cannot select or edit crop marks with the Selection tool. Expression Design does not allow you to select or reposition the crop marks with the Selection tool. To make a change to the crop marks, you must repeat the steps described here, or apply the steps described in the "Enter Settings in the Set Crop Marks Dialog Box" task or the "Set Crop Marks from Bounding Box" task.

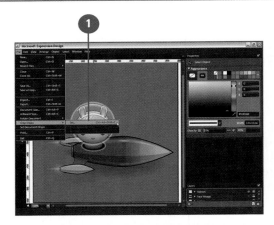

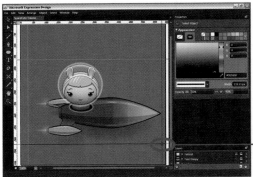

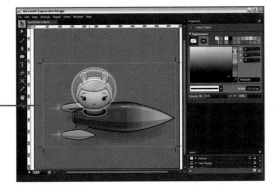

Crop Marks ——

Enter Settings in the Set Crop Marks Dialog Box

1. With a document open, select **Crop Marks** from the **File** menu, and choose **Set** from the fly-out submenu.

   TIMESAVER *Press Ctrl+Alt+Shift+C to apply the Set command quickly.*

2. Click once anywhere on the artboard to display the Set Crop Marks dialog box. Enter the preferred **X** and **Y** coordinates in the **From** and **To** fields. Use the document rulers to identify where the crop marks should be placed. Click **OK**.

   Expression Design adds the crop marks to the document.

> **Did You Know?**
>
> **The Set Crop Marks dialog box uses the same measurement units that are specified in the Units and Grids Options.** The same measurement units that appear in the rulers are what also appear in the From and To X and Y fields of the Set Crop Marks dialog box.

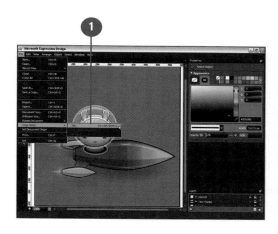

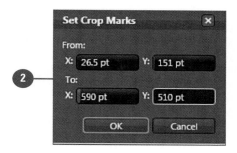

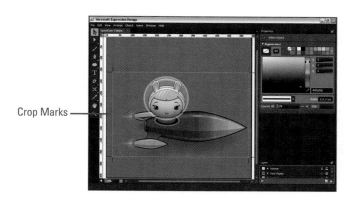

Crop Marks

Set Crop Marks from Bounding Box

1 Using any of the selection tools (Selection, Direct Selection, Lasso Selection, or Group Select), select the objects in the document that you'd like to print or export.

2 Select **Crop Marks** from the **File** menu, and choose **From Bounding Box** from the fly-out submenu.

3 Expression Design displays a Set Crop Marks dialog box that informs you what the exact coordinates and measurements of the bounding box are. It also allows you to apply an extra border width. To include extra space around the object when printing or exporting the document, enter a measurement into the **Extra Border Width** field and click **OK**.

Expression Design adds the crop marks to the document.

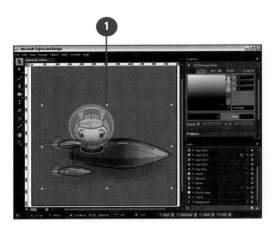

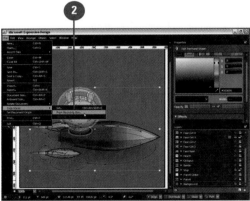

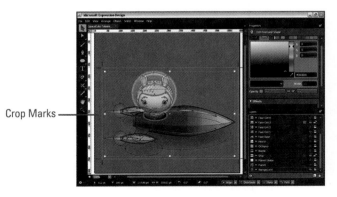

Crop Marks

Remove Crop Marks

① Open an Expression Design document that already has crop marks defined.

② Select **Crop Marks** from the **File** menu, and choose **Remove** from the fly-out submenu.

Expression Design removes the crop marks from the document.

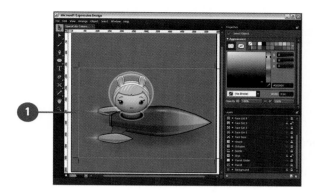

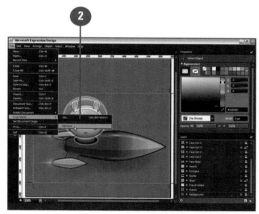

Crop Marks Removed

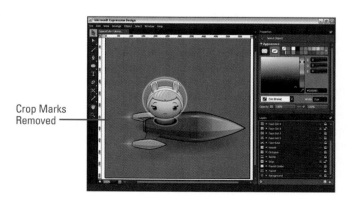

Using Pixel Preview

Expression Design's Pixel Preview feature can simulate onscreen what the document will look like when exported in a specific bitmap file format, such as GIF, JPEG, PNG, or TIFF. The Pixel Preview dialog allows you to apply all the same options as the Export dialog, without actually exporting the file. You can toggle Pixel Preview on and off by choosing the command under the View menu. To edit Pixel Preview settings while viewing the document in Pixel Preview mode, choose Change Pixel Preview Settings from the View menu.

Apply Pixel Preview

1 Open the document that you'd like to preview in a simulated bitmap format, and choose **Pixel Preview** from the **View** menu.

> **TIMESAVER** *Press Ctrl+Alt+Y to apply Pixel Preview quickly.*

2 Expression Design displays the Pixel Preview dialog box. Under the **Rasterization** settings, enter the preferred **Width, Height,** and **Resolution** settings into the respective fields. (The current document size and resolution settings are entered by default.)

> **IMPORTANT** *By entering different Width, Height, and Resolution settings in the Pixel Preview dialog box, you can simulate what the document will look like when scaled and exported at a specific resolution. These settings are not actually applied to the document.*

3 Choose a file format from the **File Type** list. Additional File Format options vary depending on which file type you choose. After applying the preferred settings, click **OK.**

Using these settings, Expression Design simulates onscreen what the document will look like when you export it.

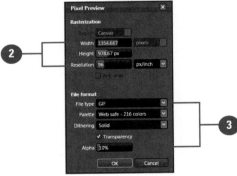

Preview Image

Printing a Document

You can send an Expression Design file to any printer that is connected to your network. However, before applying the Print command, you should always choose the proper Print and Export options and understand the settings in the Print Rasterization Settings dialog box.

Set Print Options

1 Under the **Edit** menu, select **Options** and then choose **Print and Export** from the fly-out submenu.

2 In the Options dialog box that appears, enable any of the following options:

- ◆ **Refit Curves to Output Paths**— By enabling this option, you allow Expression Design to output vector artwork much faster by not forcing it to map every node in the document. As a result, the printed artwork is perceptually very similar but not exactly the same.

- ◆ **Split Long Paths**—By splitting extremely long or complex paths into simpler paths, you can output vector artwork much faster, without affecting its visual appearance.

- ◆ **Path Quality**—By default, Expression Design applies the **Best** path quality option. However, by selecting **Draft** or **Normal** from the list, you can reduce the output quality of the artwork in exchange for faster print speeds.

- ◆ **Information Vectorization Levels**—Enter a value from 1 to 16 (the default is 5) to determine the level of information to use when vectorizing strokes based on bitmap images. This is similar to working with the Auto Trace Image command described in Chapter 10, "Working with Bitmap Images."

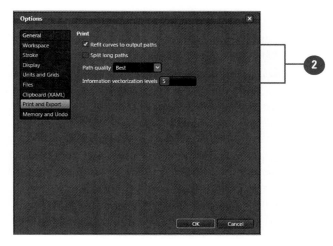

Apply the Print Command

① Open the document that you'd like to print, and choose **Print** from the **File** menu.

TIMESAVER *Press Ctrl+P to apply the Print command quickly.*

② Expression Design displays the standard Windows Print dialog box. Here you can access specific settings associated with the chosen printer's driver. The options available in this dialog box can vary from printer to printer. After you choose the proper settings, press **OK.**

③ Expression Design displays the Print Rasterization Settings dialog box, which contains the following options:

◆ **Rasterization DPI**—When printing, Expression Design always rasterizes your document (converts vector paths into pixels). Select a resolution setting in dots per inch (dpi) from the DPI list. Higher resolution settings produce better quality prints.

◆ **Print Cropmark Region**—If the document contains crop marks, you can choose to print only the area within those marks by enabling this option.

◆ **Center Page**—By enabling this option, you can print the document with the artwork centered on the page. By keeping it disabled (the default setting) the artwork is placed in the upper-left corner of the page. Refer to the dialog box preview image as a guide.

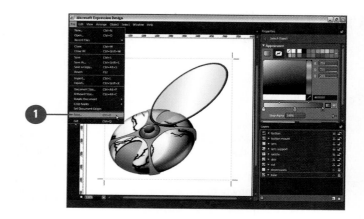

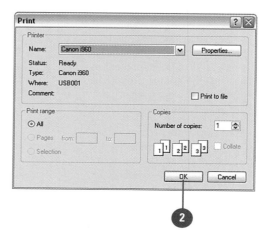

Exporting as XAML

Export Canvas

① Open the document that you'd like to export, and choose **Export** from the **File** menu.

② In the Export dialog box, choose a location to save the file. Enter a name for the document in the **File Name** field.

③ Choose the **XAML** file type from the **Save As Type** list and click **Save**.

④ In the Export XAML dialog box, click the toggle arrow next to Document Format to reveal the export options. Select **Canvas** and choose one of the following:

◆ **Export Editable TextBlocks**— Choose this option to allow the exported text to remain editable.

◆ **Export Flattened Paths**—Choose this option to convert all exported text objects to vector paths.

⑤ Click the toggle arrow next to Effects to reveal the following options:

◆ **Rasterize Live Effects**—Enable this option to convert all live effects into bitmapped images. If you choose to disable this option, some live effects might export as solid lines or fills.

◆ **Vectorize Image Strokes**— Enable this option to convert bitmap brushstrokes into overlapping vector objects. Small levels simplify strokes.

⑥ Click **Export**.

You can export your artwork in the native Expression language format, known as XAML (Extensible Application Markup Language). The Export XAML dialog box contains three different export format options: Canvas, which allows you to edit the exported objects in other XAML applications, such as Expression Blend; Silverlight, which creates a file compatible with Silverlight applications; and Resource Dictionary, which creates a collection of reusable assets.

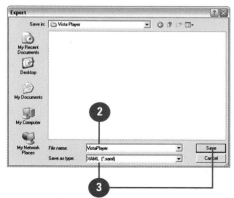

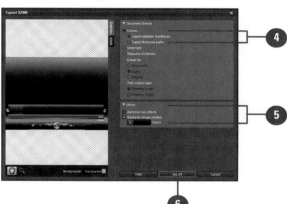

Export Silverlight

1. Open the document that you'd like to export, and choose **Export** from the **File** menu.

2. In the Export dialog box, choose a location to save the file. Enter a name for the document in the **File Name** field.

3. Choose the **XAML** file type from the **Save As Type** list and click **Save**.

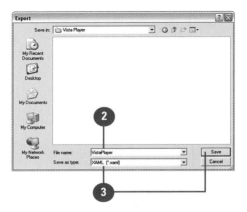

4. In the Export XAML dialog box, click the toggle arrow next to Document Format to reveal the export options. Select **Silverlight** to create a file suitable for display using an application built for Microsoft Silverlight.

5. Choose the preferred Effects export options, as described previously in the "Export Canvas" task.

6. Click **Export.**

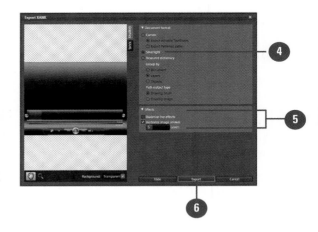

Did You Know?

Microsoft Silverlight is a cross-browser, cross-platform plug-in. Silverlight allows you to display cross-platform media, including video, animations, and interactive applications across the web.

Export Resource Dictionary

1 Open the document that you'd like to export, and choose **Export** from the **File** menu.

2 In the Export dialog box, choose a location to save the file. Enter a name for the document in the **File Name** field.

3 Choose the **XAML** file type from the **Save As Type** list and click **Save**.

4 In the Export XAML dialog box, click the toggle arrow next to Document Format to reveal the export options. Select **Resource Dictionary** to export a collection of reusable assets. Choose from the following options:

◆ **Group By**—The Document option creates a single resource for the document. Layers generates a separate resource for each layer in the document. Objects generates a separate resource for each object in the document.

◆ **Path Output Type**—The Drawing Brush option creates paths that can be used inside XAML wherever a brush type can be used. The Drawing Image option creates paths that must be wrapped inside a brush but are faster to render.

5 Choose the preferred Effects export options, as described previously in the "Export Canvas" task.

6 Click **Export**.

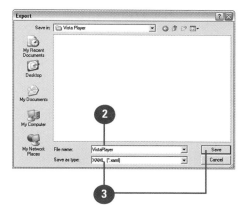

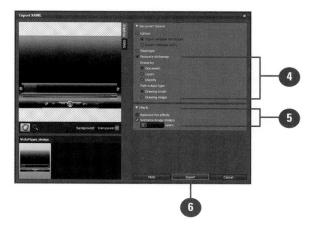

Exporting as JPEG

The JPEG file format is commonly used for saving web graphics. Expression Design allows you to determine the overall file size and image quality when exporting a document as a JPEG. You can export graphics created in Expression Design as JPEG and then use them as assets in any of your Expression Web projects.

Choose JPEG Export Options

1. Open the document that you'd like to export, and choose **Export** from the **File** menu.

2. In the Export dialog box, choose a location to save the file. Enter a name for the document in the **File Name** field.

3. Choose **JPEG** from the **Save As Type** list and click **Save**.

4. Expression Design displays the Export JPG dialog box. Under the **Rasterization** settings, enter the preferred **Width, Height,** and **Resolution** settings into the respective fields. (The current document size and resolution settings are entered by default.)

5. Enable the **Anti-Alias** option to smooth the edges of the image.

6. Select a **Quality** setting from the list provided. This option determines how accurately the document's color will be maintained upon export and how large the file size will be. Lower Quality settings produce JPEG files that contain more artifacts but are smaller in file size.

7. To embed an ICC color profile inside the exported JPEG image, enable the **Save Profile** option.

8. Click **OK** to export the file.

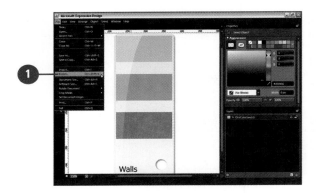

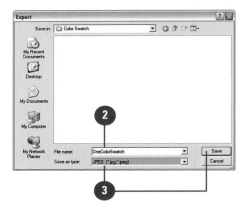

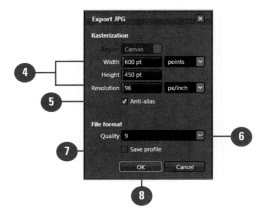

Exporting as TIFF

The TIFF file format is commonly used for saving print graphics. When exporting a document as a TIFF, Expression Design allows you to determine the color palette (Indexed Color, 24-Bit RGB, or transparent 32-Bit RGBA) and the compression setting (LZW, ZIP, or None).

Choose TIFF Export Options

1. Open the document that you'd like to export, and choose **Export** from the **File** menu.

2. In the Export dialog box, choose a system location to save the file. Enter a name for the document in the **File Name** field.

3. Choose **TIFF** from the **Save As Type** list and click **Save.**

4. Expression Design displays the Export TIFF dialog box. Enter the preferred **Width, Height,** and **Resolution** settings into the respective fields. (The current document size and resolution settings are entered by default.)

5. Enable the **Anti-Alias** option to smooth the edges of the image.

6. To specify a color palette, select a **Mode** setting from the list provided. For more information about these options, see the following "Exporting as GIF " and "Exporting as PNG" tasks.

7. Choose a compression type from the list provided. Options include LZW, ZIP, or None.

   IMPORTANT *LZW and ZIP compression are both lossless algorithms and therefore will not degrade your image.*

8. To embed an ICC color profile inside the exported TIFF image, enable the **Save Profile** option.

9. Click **OK** to export the file.

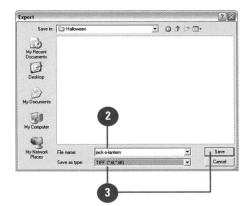

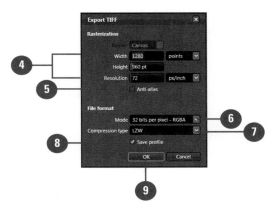

Exporting as GIF

The GIF file format is also commonly used for web graphics. Expression Design allows you to specify the color palette, dithering, and transparency options when exporting a document as a GIF. You can export graphics created in Expression Design as GIFs and then use them as assets in any of your Expression Web projects.

Choose GIF Export Options

① Open the document that you'd like to export, and choose **Export** from the **File** menu.

② In the Export dialog box, choose a system location to save the file. Enter a name for the document in the **File Name** field.

③ Choose **GIF** from the **Save As Type** list and click **Save**.

④ Expression Design displays the Export GIF dialog box. Enter the preferred **Width, Height,** and **Resolution** settings into the respective fields. (The current document settings are entered by default.)

⑤ Enable the **Anti-Alias** option to smooth the edges of the image.

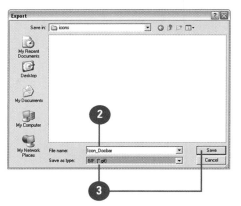

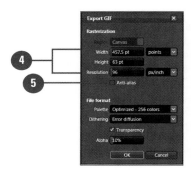

6 Select a **Palette** setting from the list provided. This option lets you specify a color palette for the image.

◆ **Web Safe** uses a standard palette of 216 colors that 8-bit monitors can display without dithering.

◆ **Optimized** picks the most common 256 colors in the image.

◆ **Grayscale** uses 256 levels of gray.

7 Choose a **Dithering** option from the list provided.

◆ **Error Diffusion** simulates colors that do not match the chosen color palette exactly.

◆ **Solid** disables dithering and maps all colors to their nearest palette equivalent.

8 When choosing Web Safe or Optimized Palette options, you can also choose to maintain any transparent areas by enabling the **Transparency** option. By setting a percentage with the **Alpha** slider, you can specify how transparent an image area must be to appear fully transparent in the exported GIF.

IMPORTANT *Image areas in a GIF file can either be fully transparent or fully opaque, but not partially transparent. To export partially transparent areas, you should export the image in the PNG file format.*

9 Click **OK** to export the file.

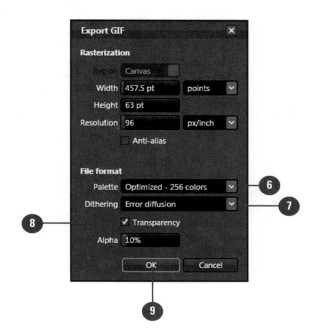

Exporting as PNG

If the graphics that you'd like to export contain partial transparency, the PNG format is a much better export option than GIF, which does not allow you to export partially transparent pixels. The PNG file format allows you to export in 32-Bit RGBA mode (the "A" stands for alpha transparency), whereas the GIF file format does not.

Choose PNG Export Options

1 Open the document that you'd like to export, and choose **Export** from the **File** menu.

2 In the Export dialog box, choose a location to save the file. Enter a name for the document in the **File Name** field.

3 Choose **PNG** from the **Save As Type** list and click **Save**.

4 Expression Design displays the Export PNG dialog box. Enter the preferred **Width, Height,** and **Resolution** settings into the respective fields. (The current document settings are entered by default.)

5 Enable the **Anti-Alias** option to smooth the edges of the image.

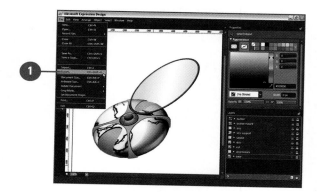

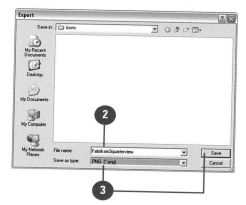

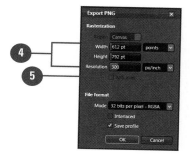

6 Select a **Mode** setting from the list provided. This option lets you specify a color palette for the image.

- ◆ **Indexed Color** limits the number of colors to 256. You can control the color mapping for Indexed Color by choosing **Palette**, **Dithering**, and **Transparency** options as described in the "Exporting as GIF" task.

- ◆ **24-Bit RGB** creates an RGB image with no transparency.

- ◆ **32-Bit RGBA** creates an RGB image with full alpha transparency.

7 To allow the PNG to appear in a web browser with interlacing (to display gradually from coarse to fine), enable the **Interlaced** option.

8 To embed an ICC color profile inside the exported PNG image, enable the **Save Profile** option.

9 Click **OK** to export the file.

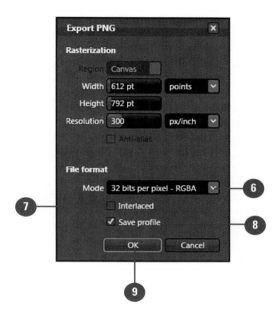

Exporting as PDF

The controls in the Export PDF dialog box allow you to determine how Expression Design should handle certain items that the PDF format does not support, such as transparent gradients, brushstrokes based on bitmap images, and live effects. To ensure that these items appear correctly in the exported PDF, you should choose to rasterize them (convert them to pixel-based, bitmap images).

Choose PDF Export Options

① Open the document that you'd like to export, and choose **Export** from the **File** menu.

② In the Export dialog box, choose a location to save the file. Enter a name for the document in the **File Name** field.

③ Choose **PDF** from the **Save As Type** list and click **Save**.

④ Expression Design displays the Export PDF dialog box. In the **Rasterization** section of the dialog box, you can choose to rasterize any **Transparent Gradients**, **Image Strokes**, and **Live Effects** into bitmap images. If you choose not to enable any of these options, some of these items might export as solid lines or fills.

⑤ Enter a value from 1 to 16 (the default is 5) in the **Levels** field to determine the level of information to use when vectorizing strokes based on bitmap images. This is similar to working with the Auto Trace Image command described in Chapter 10, "Working with Bitmap Images."

⑥ Click **OK** to export the file.

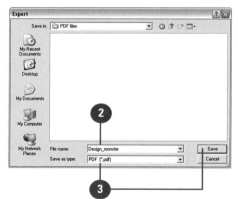

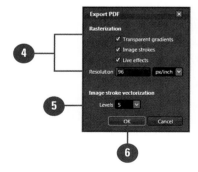

Exporting to Adobe Photoshop

Expression Design allows you to export your graphics into the native Adobe Photoshop format (PSD, or Photoshop Document). You can choose to export a PSD in either 24-Bit RGB mode or the transparent 32-Bit RGBA mode. When exporting a PSD in 24-Bit RGB mode, all Expression Design layers are flattened into a single layer in the Photoshop file; when exporting in 32-Bit RGBA mode, you have the option to convert Expression Design layers into Photoshop layers.

Choose PSD Export Options

1. Open the document that you'd like to export, and choose **Export** from the **File** menu.

2. In the Export dialog box, choose a system location to save the file. Enter a name for the document in the **File Name** field.

3. Choose **Adobe Photoshop** from the **Save As Type** list and click **Save.**

4. Expression Design displays the Export PSD dialog box. Enter the preferred **Width, Height,** and **Resolution** settings into the respective fields. (The current document settings are entered by default.)

5. Enable the **Anti-Alias** option to smooth the edges of the image.

6. Select a **Mode** setting from the list provided.

   ◆ **24-Bit RGB** creates an RGB image with no transparency.

   ◆ **32-Bit RGBA** creates an RGB image with full alpha transparency.

7. If you choose to export in the 32-Bit RGBA mode, the **Save Layers** option appears. Enable this option to export the Expression Design layer information into the PSD.

8. Click **OK** to export the file.

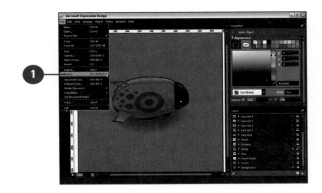

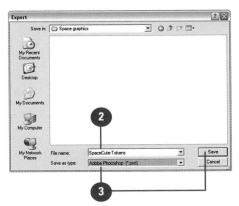

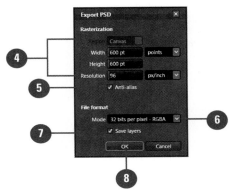

Exporting as BMP

The BMP file format is commonly used to create graphics for use with Microsoft Office applications. When exporting a document as a BMP, Expression Design allows you to determine the size, resolution, and the color mode (Indexed Color, 24-Bit RGB, or transparent 32-Bit RGBA).

Choose BMP Export Options

1. Open the document that you'd like to export, and choose **Export** from the **File** menu.

2. In the Export dialog box, choose a location to save the file. Enter a name for the document in the **File Name** field.

3. Choose **BMP** from the **Save As Type** list and click **Save**.

4. Expression Design displays the Export BMP dialog box. Under the **Rasterization** settings, enter the preferred **Width, Height,** and **Resolution** settings into the respective fields. (The current document size and resolution settings are entered by default.)

5. Enable the **Anti-Alias** option to smooth the edges of the image.

6. To specify a color palette, select a **Mode** setting from the list provided. For more information about these options, see the previous "Exporting as PNG" and "Exporting as GIF" tasks.

7. Click **OK** to export the file.

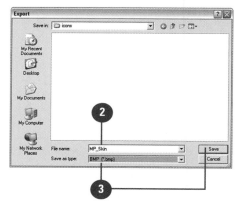

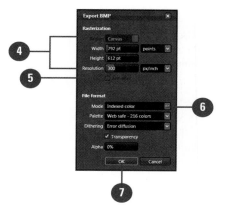

Exporting as Windows Media Photo

Choose WDP Export Options

When exporting a document as a Windows Media Photo (WDP) file, you have the option to save it in 24-Bit RGB mode or transparent 32-Bit RGBA mode. You can also choose to apply lossless compression to the image, similar to exporting as a TIFF.

① Open the document that you'd like to export, and choose **Export** from the **File** menu.

② In the Export dialog box, choose a location to save the file. Enter a name for the document in the **File Name** field.

③ Choose **Windows Media Photo** from the **Save As Type** list and click **Save**.

④ Expression Design displays the Export Windows Media Photo dialog box. Enter the preferred **Width, Height,** and **Resolution** settings into the respective fields. (The current document size and resolution settings are entered by default.)

⑤ Enable the **Anti-Alias** option to smooth the edges of the image.

⑥ Select a **Mode** setting:

◆ **24-Bit RGB** creates an RGB image with no transparency.

◆ **32-Bit RGBA** creates an RGB image with full alpha transparency.

⑦ Enable the **Lossless** option to apply lossless compression to the image. Doing so reduces the file size while maintaining as much image quality as possible.

⑧ Specify the amount of quality that you'd like to maintain by adjusting the Quality slider.

⑨ Click **OK** to export the file.

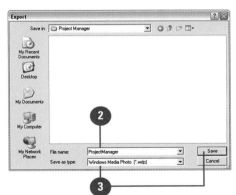

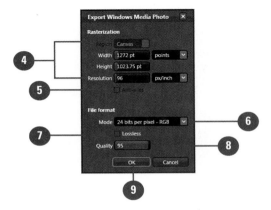

Index